A BASIC SYSTEMS PROGRAM

REFLEX AND OPERANT CONDITIONING

George L. Geis
Center for Research on Learning and Teaching
University of Michigan

William C. Stebbins
Kresge Hearing Research Institute
University of Michigan

Robert W. Lundin
Chairman, Department of Psychology
University of the South

with Epilogues by Fred S. Keller,
Professor of Psychology
University of Arizona

The Study of Behavior
Volume 1—Parts 1, 2

Appleton-Century-Crofts
Division of Meredith Publishing Company
New York

Copyright © 1965 by

BASIC SYSTEMS, INC.

PRINTED IN THE UNITED STATES OF AMERICA

655–1

Dedication

*To our students
who are patiently teaching us
to write better programs*

Preface

This programmed text was originally developed under a grant to Hamilton College by the Fund for the Advancement of Education of the Ford Foundation. This grant supported the development and testing of an entire program, designed for use in a first-year course in systematic psychology at the college level. The present volume was adapted from the first portion of that course, and represents the first publication for wider use of what is planned as a complete course.

Each unit of the program was used and validated in the introductory course at Hamilton College. Portions of the program, including that portion here published, have undergone repeated testing and revision under such conditions of use. The material in the present volume was further tested by Basic Systems, Inc., with selected groups of students drawn from classes at Barnard, Columbia, Fairleigh Dickinson, and Hunter Colleges. The final revision has been validated with freshman and sophomore students at Columbia's School of General Studies, and with introductory psychology students, as well as non-psychology postgraduates, at the University of Michigan. To the many students who provided data used in revising the program, and the instructors who helped us recruit and select these students, our thanks are due.

A description of the validation procedure, and the results obtained in testing, are available to teachers and researchers from the Programming Department, Appleton-Century-Crofts —— 440 Park Avenue South, New York, N.Y. 10016.

In the space provided we cannot adequately thank the many people who have contributed to this volume and to the series. A few names may serve as a sample, however. We express our deep appreciation to:

Mrs. Lawrence Yourtee, who typed and retyped literally thousands of pages of manuscript revisions.

Mr. Charles Peyser, who for several years was research assistant on the project.

Dr. Donald A. Cook and Mr. Stephen F. Knapp of Basic Systems, Inc., who aided in the substantial editing and revision of this volume.

The Fund for the Advancement of Education of the Ford Foundation, whose original sponsorship made the project possible.

Professor Fred S. Keller, whose teaching serves as a continual reminder of what a program should try to achieve.

To the Teacher

This programmed textbook is designed to impart, in brief but intensive compass, a grasp of the basic principles of the acquisition of behavior. The first section is devoted to reflexes and reflex conditioning, as studied and brought into the realm of scientific psychology by Ivan Pavlov. The second section takes up operant behavior and its strengthening; this section takes its departure from B. F. Skinner's formulation of the law of operant conditioning.

Reflexes and Conditioned Reflexes

The treatment in this section emphasizes an accurate description of the behavioral relations involved in studying reflex and the formation of new reflexes through the pairing of stimuli. In achieving this aim, the student is exposed to the practical use of certain concepts of wide application in the scientific study of behavior; examples are the notions of *threshold* and *latency,* and their treatment as dependent variables, in a functional approach which emphasizes the relation between independent and dependent variables.

It is our contention as authors of the program that the distinction between classical or Pavlovian (reflex) conditioning and operant (or instrumental) conditioning is a valid one and a very important first principle for an introductory course in psychology. Further, we feel that there is good evidence that this distinction between the types of conditioning is directly related to the physiologic difference between the autonomic and somatic systems. Consequently, in the treatment of reflex conditioning practically all the examples of reflexes are autonomic and involve innervation of smooth muscle, gland, or cardiac muscle. We feel that reported instances of classical defense conditioning (e.g., foot withdrawal, finger withdrawal, eye blink, etc.) may be examples of operant conditioning (i.e., avoidance). However, the use of the program does not in any way preclude the instructor from presenting additional material on reflexes of his own choosing.

Operant Conditioning

The presentation of operant behavior and its conditioning is limited to the simplest exposition of a few principles. Since the emphasis is upon the *acquisition* of behavior, topics such as extinction, and the maintenance of behavior through schedules of reinforcement, have been avoided. Similarly, extensions to more complex topics such as discrimination, secondary reinforcement, and punishment have been left aside. It is our intention to devote a full volume to each of these and to other important variables in the study of behavior.

On the other hand, an introductory treatment of the differentiation of behavior ("shaping") has been included, to complete the account of the acquisition of behavior by showing how *new* behavior can be brought into being through reinforcement. Furthermore, escape conditioning, often reserved for later treatment, is here given a chapter of its own, since it is properly classed with the basic account of acquisition. Attention is called to a novel paradigm which has been developed to stress that the reinforcing contingency in escape behavior is the removal of an aversive stimulus; the aversive stimulus precedes the response, but its removal is a consequence of the response, and it is this change which is reinforcing. The paradigm brings out both aspects of the case.

In the interests of rigor and brevity, certain topics of historical interest have been passed over. Thorndike's Cats in a Puzzle Box, and the large literature of maze learning, are viewed as requiring advanced concepts—such as secondary reinforcement, discrimination, and chaining—to give a satisfactory account. The instructor interested in historical perspective may well wish to discuss, or assign readings in, such topics.

The program can appropriately be assigned in the early weeks of general or advanced general courses, as well as more specialized courses in learning, comparative psychology, or educational psychology. Two examinations will be found at the end of the volume, designed to cover two major concepts and principles taught by the program. The first examination covers *Reflexes and Conditioned Reflexes* alone. The second, while emphasizing operant behavior, also tests knowledge of the main distinctions between the two forms of conditioning. The instructor facing a class of mixed degree of preparation may wish to employ these tests as screening devices for selective assignment of the program. More often, he may wish to use them as pretests before assigning the program, and as posttests afterwards, for the purposes of evaluating gains and motivating the student. Test results, based on either a single administration, or use before and after the program, may also be used as the basis for review, discussion, and clarification.

To the Student

About Psychology

Psychology is the study of behavior. It deals with the effects of the environment upon an organism, be he man or mouse. The purpose of this program is to start you on a scientific account of the relationships between the behavior of organisms and the surrounding environment. When you have completed this program you should be able to apply some of the principles to familiar examples from your experience. You will probably have many questions about areas with which the program does not deal, and working with the program itself will raise other questions. If this program helps you to phrase those questions more carefully and exactly, one of its main purposes will have been well served.

About the Use of This Program

This program is designed to guide you through the subject in a careful sequence of steps which makes for efficient learning. Each step is called a "frame," and each frame brings in something new. It also asks you to use this new material—which is carefully based on what you have already learned—in an *active response*. This means that you will be asked to complete a sentence, fill in a blank, check a multiple-choice question, label a drawing, or make some other brief response. It is best to make your response in the space provided in the frame itself. Do not use the length of the blank as a cue to the length of your answer. Sometimes you will need to write a phrase in a single blank. After you have made your response, you can check your answer with the correct answer which is next to each frame. Thus you will master the material in a step-by-step fashion, responding to each step, and checking each answer you write.

The frames of the program—which contain the material to study and the questions to answer—are on the left-hand side of each page, and are numbered in serial order. The answer to each frame is just to its right, and is printed in a shaded column to help you avoid glancing at the answer before you write your own. Does it matter if you peek at the answer before you try your own? Yes, it does—you will not learn as well. This program has been tried out on many students, and revised on the basis of their results. We know, therefore, that you will get most frames right on your own, and that if you write your answer to each one, you will learn well. Many students find it helpful to cover the answer with an index card, which you can slide down the answer column as you progress through the frames.

Despite our efforts, and yours, you will probably make an occasional error. When this happens, check the answer given and satisfy yourself that you understand it. If you think it better than yours, correct your own response before proceeding.

The program is organized into relatively brief chapters. Each one may take you anywhere from half an hour to an hour to complete, and it is best to work on the program when you can complete an entire chapter at one sitting.

Remember: You will learn in steps, respond to each step, and check your answer right away—*after* your response! This is not a test and there are no trick questions. After mastering this program in the proper manner, you will understand some important principles of psychology.

At the back of this program, you will notice several panels. You will be asked to respond to the material contained in them. These panels contain critical information which, because of length and/or complexity, cannot be included in the body of the program. Note also that these panels are perforated to facilitate their removal and use.

As you take the program, you will be required to refer to these panels. The directions at these points will be in a form such as "REFER TO PANEL A." When required to refer to a panel, tear it out and use it until directed otherwise.

Contents

Part 1

REFLEXES AND CONDITIONED REFLEXES

Reflexes

1

Things happen in our *environment*. For example:

    a. Juicy steak is placed on the tongue.

    b. A light is shined in the eye.

These things that happen affect our *behavior* in certain ways. For example:

    c. Saliva flows in the mouth.

    d. Pupil of the eye becomes smaller.

The placing of steak in the mouth probably is followed by:

    ☒ saliva flow

    ☐ decrease in size of the pupil

Shining a light in the eye is followed by:

    ☐ saliva flow

    ☒ decrease in size of the pupil

saliva flow

decrease in size of the pupil

- -

2

An event in the environment is called a *stimulus* (plural *stimuli*). Parts of our behavior are called *responses*.

The increase of temperature in a room is a:

    ☒ stimulus

    ☐ response

This leads to perspiring, which is a:

    ☐ stimulus

    ☒ response

stimulus

response

- -

3

Which is the stimulus?
- ☒ cold wind
- ☐ weeping

Which is the response?
- ☒ "goose pimples" appear
- ☐ onion placed under nose

cold wind

"goose pimples" appear

- -

4

Psychologists are interested when stimuli and responses are *related* in some way.

CHECK the sentence that seems to express a relationship between stimulus and response:
- ☐ As he walked down the hill, a cool wind began to blow.
- ☒ As the cool wind blew, "goose pimples" appeared on his arms.

As the cool wind blew, goose pimples appeared on his arms.

- -

5

This relationship between a stimulus and a response is called a *reflex*. Here is an example:

If a light shines in your eye, the pupil contracts (becomes smaller).

In this reflex, the stimulus is the _____ and the response is the _____ of the _____.

light
contraction (of the) pupil

- -

6

In describing this reflex, we say that:

Light elicits pupil contraction.

The subject of this sentence is the name of a:
- ☐ stimulus
- ☐ response

stimulus

- -

7

To *elicit* means "to draw out, to draw forth, to bring forth." The word *elicit* is a(n):

☐ noun
☐ verb
☐ adjective

verb

8

Here is another example of a reflex:

An onion placed under the nose causes tears to flow.

The response in this reflex is _____.

weeping *or* flow of tears

9

An onion placed under the nose causes tears to flow from the eyes.

In this reflex, the onion is a(n) _____.

The weeping is a(n) _____.

stimulus
response

10

A rotten odor elicits vomiting.

What word in the sentence tells that the stimulus and response are related in a reflex? _____

elicits

11

If you receive an electric shock, your heart rate may increase.

WRITE a sentence using the following terms:

elicits
electric shock
heart rate increase

Electric shock elicits heart rate increase.

12

Light "brings forth" pupil contraction.
REPLACE the phrase *brings forth* with the correct technical term. _____

elicits

- -

13

The general description of a reflex is:

A(n) _____ elicits a(n) _____.

stimulus   response

- -

14

CHECK the appropriate response for each of the following stimuli:

Stimuli	*Responses*
Steak on the tongue elicits:	☐ tears
	☐ pupil contraction
	☐ salivation
An onion under the nose elicits:	☐ tears
	☐ pupil contraction
	☐ salivation

salivation

tears

- -

15

Steak in the mouth does *not* elicit: (CHECK ONE)
- ☐ salivation
- ☐ weeping

weeping

- -

16

What technical term do we use to describe the relationship between stimulus and response in a reflex? (Hint: The term is a verb meaning "to draw out, to draw forth, to bring forth.")

_____

to elicit *or* elicit *or* elicits

- -

17

CHECK the stimulus that would elicit each of the following two responses:

    Heart rate increase:
        ☐ light
        ☐ an onion
        ☐ shock

    Pupil contraction:
        ☐ light
        ☐ an onion
        ☐ shock

shock

light

- - - - - - - - - - - - - - - - - - - -

18

Light does *not* elicit:
    ☐ heart rate increase
    ☐ pupil contraction

heart rate increase

- - - - - - - - - - - - - - - - - - - -

19

To predict what response will be elicited in a reflex, it helps if you know what _____ was presented.

stimulus

- - - - - - - - - - - - - - - - - - - -

20

In a reflex, a specific stimulus elicits its own particular _____.

response

- - - - - - - - - - - - - - - - - - - -

21

In a reflex, a stimulus _____ a response.

elicits

- - - - - - - - - - - - - - - - - - - -

22

Does a light normally elicit weeping?

☐ yes

☐ no

no

Does the relationship between light and weeping normally make up a reflex?

☐ yes

☐ no

no

- -

23

Do any stimulus and any response form a reflex?

☐ yes

☐ no

no

- -

24

Only when a stimulus elicits a response can we speak of a(n) _____.

reflex

- -

25

A freezing temperature _____ shivering.

elicits

This relationship between stimulus and response is called a(n) _____.

reflex

- -

26

When a specific _____ elicits a(n) _____, the relationship is called a(n) _____.

stimulus

response

reflex

- -

27

When a stimulus elicits a response, which comes first in time?

☐ the stimulus

☐ the response

the stimulus

- -

28

When we speak of a *reflex*, the two things we observe are the _____ and the _____.

stimulus   response

- -

29

To discover whether a particular stimulus is an eliciting stimulus for a given reflex, we present the stimulus and observe whether the _____ occurs.

response

- -

30

If the stimulus elicits the response, the relationship of stimulus and response is called a(n) _____.

reflex

- -

31

In a reflex, which comes first?
- ☐ stimulus
- ☐ response

stimulus

- -

32

We have used the word *stimuli* to describe parts of, or changes in parts of:
- ☐ behavior
- ☐ the environment

the environment

- -

33

Our technical term for parts of the environment, or changes in parts of the environment, is _____.

stimulus *or* stimuli

- -

34

A steady light can be called a stimulus because it is a:

□ part of the environment

□ change in part of the environment

A soft sound becoming loud can also be called a stimulus because it is a:

□ part of the environment

□ change in part of the environment

part of the environment

change in part of the environment

_ _

35

A stimulus is a part of, or a change in a part of, the _____.

environment

_ _

36

A part of, or a change in a part of, the *environment* is called a(n) _____.

stimulus

In like manner, a part of, or a change in a part of, *behavior* must be the definition of a(n) _____.

response

_ _

37

Stimulus is a technical term used in describing the environment.

Response is a technical term used in describing _____.

behavior

_ _

38

A stimulus is a part of, or a _____ in a part of, the environment.

change

_ _

39

A response is a _____ of, or a change in a _____ of, the behavior. (The same word goes in both blanks.)

part

part

_ _

40

When a given stimulus elicits a specific response, the relationship is called a(n) _____.

reflex

- -

41

DEFINE a *stimulus*.

_____

A stimulus is a part of, or a change in a part of, the environment.
(or equivalent answer)

- -

42

DEFINE a *response*.

_____

A response is a part of, or a change in a part of behavior.
(or equivalent answer)

- -

43

In a reflex, the first event is the presentation of the _____.

stimulus

The second event is the elicitation of the _____.

response

- -

44

In a reflex, we say that the stimulus _____ the response.

elicits

- -

45

REVIEW AND PREVIEW

You have learned some important terms and concepts. For example, you know that the psychologist analyzes the environment into more specific parts called _____.

stimuli

You also know that the psychologist analyzes behavior into more specific parts called _____.

responses

- -

46

You have become familiar with one specific relationship between stimuli and responses. That relationship exists when a stimulus elicits a response, and we call it a _____.

reflex

_____

47

In all the reflexes we have considered, the first event in time was the:

    ☐ stimulus

    ☐ response

stimulus

and the second event to occur was the:

    ☐ stimulus

    ☐ response

response

_____

48

We have used a special term to describe the relationship between the stimulus and the response in a reflex. We say:

    "In a reflex, the stimulus _____ the response."

elicits

_____

49

But we have *not* discussed "where reflexes come from." Some, for example, may be present at birth. Which reflex might you expect to find in a newborn baby?

    ☐ having "goose pimples" when hearing the national anthem

    ☐ sucking when lips and tongue are stimulated

sucking when lips and tongue are stimulated

_____

50

The reaction of having "goose pimples" when hearing the national anthem is *not* present at birth. Yet it is a reflex. The stimulus is _____ and the response is _____.

hearing national anthem

having "goose pimples"

— — — — — — — — — — — — — — — — — —

51

Given the stimulus (national anthem) and the response ("goose pimples"), there remains to be explained how the stimulus comes to _____ the response.

elicit

— — — — — — — — — — — — — — — — — —

52

When we have explained such cases, we will have some understanding of both unlearned and learned _____ (plural).

reflexes

— — — — — — — — — — — — — — — — — —

53

We know that neither kind of reflex—unlearned or learned—will occur unless we first present a(n) _____.

stimulus

— — — — — — — — — — — — — — — — — —

54

When the dinner bell rings, you may start salivating. When you taste a juicy steak, you may salivate. Which case sounds like an unlearned reflex?

☐ dinner bell rings and you salivate

☐ you taste steak and you salivate

you taste steak and you salivate

— — — — — — — — — — — — — — — — — —

55

In the foregoing example, which reflex was unlearned?

☐ salivation to steak

☐ salivation to dinner bell

salivation to steak

— — — — — — — — — — — — — — — — — —

56

Dinner bell elicits salivation.

This reflex is:

☐ unlearned

☐ learned

learned

- -

57

Generally speaking, the psychologist studies the relationship between the environment and the behavior of an organism.

The important parts of the environment, he calls _____ (plural).

stimuli

The important parts of behavior he calls _____ (plural).

responses

- -

58

Some reflex relationships between stimuli and responses are unlearned, while others are learned.

COMPLETE the entry of checks in the table below to indicate which reflexes are unlearned and which are learned:

STIMULUS	RESPONSE	TYPE OF REFLEX Unlearned	Learned		Unlearned	Learned
cinder in eye	blinking	X			(X)	
dinner bell	salivation		X			(X)
embarrassing situation	blushing					X
onion under the nose	weeping				X	
food in mouth	salivation				X	
national anthem	goose pimples					X
light in eye	pupil contraction				X	
electric shock	increase in heart rate				X	
sound of dentist's drill	sweating and trembling					X

Effective Stimuli

1

Suppose someone far across the room from you held an onion in his hand. Do you think your eyes would water?

    ☐ probably
    ☐ probably not

probably not

– –

2

As he walked toward you, the odor of the onion would become stronger. If he held the onion under your nose, you might start to weep because the odor is then:

    ☐ strong
    ☐ weak

strong

– –

3

If a stimulus is weak enough, it will fail to _____ any response.

elicit

– –

4

Which stimulus will not elicit a response?

    ☐ a strong stimulus
    ☐ a weak stimulus

a weak stimulus

– –

5

If we decrease or turn down a very intense stimulus to a low enough value, it will no longer elicit any _____.

response

– –

6

The strong odor of onion elicits weeping. A weak odor of onion *does not* elicit weeping.

What determines whether weeping occurs?
_____

the strength *or* intensity of the odor (stimulus)

- -

7

To state this question another way, we might ask: In studying the pupillary reflex, how _____ a light is required to elicit pupil contraction?

intense *or* bright *or* strong

- -

8

If we start with a weak light that elicits no response, and we make it gradually brighter and brighter, we will reach a point at which the light will _____ pupil contraction. We call that point the *threshold*.

elicit

If the intensity of a light is below the threshold, the light (□ will □ will not) elicit pupil contraction. If the intensity is above the threshold, the light (□ will □ will not) elicit pupil contraction.

will not

will

- -

9

What do we call the point at which a stimulus (light) will elicit a response (pupil contraction)?
_____

the threshold

- -

10

A stimulus below the threshold (□ will □ will not) elicit a response.

will not

- -

11

In any given reflex, the threshold refers to the intensity of a(n) _____ just sufficient to elicit a(n) _____.

stimulus

response

- -

12

If we gradually increase the intensity of a stimulus, we reach a point at which the stimulus will elicit a response. That point is known as the _____.

threshold

— — — — — — — — — — — — — — — — — — —

13

Every reflex has a threshold. If you know the threshold value, you know how intense to make the _____ in order to _____.
        (phrase)

stimulus   elicit the response

— — — — — — — — — — — — — — — — — — —

14

Suppose a light of 6 units of intensity is the least intense light that will elicit pupil contraction. The threshold for this reflex is ____ units.

6

— — — — — — — — — — — — — — — — — — —

15

The minimal value of a stimulus sufficient to elicit a response is called the _____.

threshold

— — — — — — — — — — — — — — — — — — —

16

In the previous example: If the threshold is 6 units, then a stimulus of 4 units would be (□ above the threshold □ below the threshold). Would the stimulus of 4 units elicit a response?
        □ yes
        □ no

below the threshold

no

— — — — — — — — — — — — — — — — — — —

17

And if the light were of 8 units intensity, then it would be (□ above □ below) the threshold for pupillary contraction. A light of 8 units (□ would □ would not) elicit contraction.

above
would

— — — — — — — — — — — — — — — — — — —

18

In a reflex, the threshold is the lowest intensity value of a stimulus sufficient to elicit a particular _____.

response

- -

19

DEFINE the term *threshold*. _____

Threshold is the minimal value of a stimulus sufficient to elicit a response.
(or equivalent answer)

- -

20

The word *limen* is synonymous with the word *threshold*. A stimulus of a value below the limen will not _____.

elicit a response

- -

21

If stimulus intensity is above the threshold for a given reflex, then we could also say it is:

☐ above the limen
☐ below the limen

above the limen

- -

22

A synonym for the word *threshold* is the word _____.

limen

- -

23

If *sub* means *below* and *limen* means *threshold*, then *subliminal* refers to a stimulus that is below the _____.

threshold *or* limen

- -

24

If the limen or threshold is 6 units, then a value of _____ units would be subliminal.

any number below 6

- -

25

If the limen is 6 units, then a stimulus with a value of 2 units is a(n) _____ stimulus.

subliminal

_ _

26

If *subliminal* means *below threshold,* and *supra* means *above,* what does *supraliminal* mean?
_____

above threshold *or* limen

_ _

27

If 6 units is liminal, 7 units should be _____ liminal.

supraliminal

_ _

28

Which stimulus will *not* elicit a response?
☐ subliminal
☐ supraliminal

subliminal

_ _

29

Will a supraliminal stimulus elicit a response?
☐ yes
☐ no

yes

_ _

READ THROUGH PANEL R-2-1 BEFORE GOING ON TO THE FOLLOWING ITEMS.

_ _

30

(Refer to Panel R-2-1.)

The panel reports a study on the pupillary reflex. What stimulus was used? _____

light *or* a spot of light flashed in the eye

_ _

31

(Refer to Panel R-2-1.)

The experimenter varied the (□ duration □ intensity) of the light.

intensity

32

(Refer to Panel R-2-1.)

In the dark, the diameter of the pupil is 6.5 millimeters. At 0.000001 foot-lambert of intensity or less, the diameter of the pupil is:
    □ about the same
    □ very much smaller

about the same

33

An intensity of less than 0.000001 foot-lambert of light is (□ above □ below) the threshold for the pupillary reflex.

below

34

For the pupillary reflex, a light intensity of less than 0.000001 foot-lambert is:
    □ supraliminal
    □ subliminal

subliminal

35

(Refer to Panel R-2-1.)

As the light gets brighter, what happens to the size (diameter) of the pupil? _____

The diameter of the pupil decreases.

36

(Refer to Panel R-2-1.)

At 10 foot-lamberts of intensity, the diameter of the pupil is about _____ millimeters.

3

37

The greater the intensity of the light, the more the pupil contracts. In the brightest light, the pupil is (☐ least ☐ most) contracted, and the diameter of the pupil is (☐ largest ☐ smallest).

most
smallest

_ _

38

Which produces a greater change in pupil size?
- ☐ increasing the light intensity from a subliminal value to 8 units
- ☐ increasing the light intensity from a subliminal value to 10 units

increasing the light intensity from a subliminal value to 10 units

_ _

39

In the pupillary reflex:
The stimulus is the intensity of the _____.
The contraction in pupil size is the _____.

light
response

_ _

40

The response (contraction) to light is greatest when the intensity of the stimulus is (☐ highest ☐ lowest).

highest

_ _

41

In other words, increasing the intensity of the light has what effect on the response? _____

increases the response

_ _

42

When two stimuli are both above threshold for a given reflex, the stronger stimulus will elicit a(n) _____ response.

stronger
(or equivalent answer)

_ _

43

Usually, *intensity* refers to the strength of the stimulus and *magnitude* refers to the strength of the response. Therefore, we would say that as the intensity of a stimulus is increased, the magnitude of the _____ increases.

response

- -

44

In general, the magnitude of the response is dependent on the intensity of the _____.

stimulus

- -

45

One measure of a response is its magnitude. The magnitude of the response is directly related to the _____ of the _____.

intensity (of the) stimulus

- -

46

The _____ of a response is related to the intensity of the stimulus that elicits it.

magnitude

- -

47

We measure the salivary response in terms of the quantity of saliva elicited. This is a measure of the _____ of the response.

magnitude

- -

48

In the pupillary reflex, the magnitude of the response (the extent of the pupil contraction) will depend on the _____ of the light stimulus.

intensity

- -

49

Increasing the light intensity will have what effect on the response? _____

It will increase the magnitude of the response.

- -

50

If there is a decrease in the _____ of the light stimulus, there will be a(n) _____ in the magnitude of the pupil contraction (response).

intensity
decrease

_____

51

The _____ of the elicited response is dependent upon the _____ of the _____.

magnitude
intensity (of the) stimulus

_____

52

If an experimenter increases the intensity of the stimulus, the magnitude of the elicited response:
- ☐ increases
- ☐ decreases

increases

If the experimenter decreases stimulus intensity, the response magnitude:
- ☐ increases
- ☐ decreases

decreases

_____

53

Every reflex has a threshold. A stimulus whose intensity is below the threshold:
- ☐ will elicit the response
- ☐ will not elicit the response

will not elicit the response

A supraliminal stimulus:
- ☐ will elicit the response
- ☐ will not elicit the response

will elicit the response

_____

54

A stimulus above threshold for a given reflex can also be called _____.

supraliminal

Increasing the intensity of such a stimulus will generally increase the _____ of the response.

magnitude

_____

Measuring Reflex Strength:
Latency and Magnitude

1

It is possible to change the (□ intensity □ magnitude) of a supraliminal stimulus. Such a change changes the (□ intensity □ magnitude) of the response.

intensity

magnitude

— —

2

The magnitude of the response varies with the _____ of the _____.

intensity (of the) stimulus

— —

3

Which response has the longer time between the presentation of the stimulus and the occurrence of the response?

    □ *a.* Salivation begins 4 seconds after the food touches the tongue.

    □ *b.* Pupil contraction begins 1/10 second after light shines in the eye.

a.

The time between the presentation of the stimulus and the occurrence of the response is called the *latency* of the response.

What is the latency in each of the two examples above?

    a. _____ second(s).
    b. _____ second(s).

4 (seconds)
1/10 (second)

— —

4

The greater the amount of time elapsing between stimulus and response, the (□ longer □ shorter) is the latency.

longer

— —

5

The latency of a response is the elapsed _____ between the stimulus and the response.

time

– –

6

The latency of a response is the time between the presentation of the _____ and the occurrence of a _____.

stimulus
response

– –

7

The elapsed time between the onset of a stimulus and the initiation of a response is called the _____.

latency

– –

8

Picture the second hand on a watch or clock. A light is turned on when the hand is at 30 seconds; the subject's pupil begins to contract at 31 seconds. The latency of pupillary contraction would be _____ (two words).

one second

– –

9

Suppose that we record the time when lemon juice is put on a subject's tongue. Then we record the time when the first drop of saliva occurs. The difference between these two times is the _____ of the salivary response.

latency

– –

10

DEFINE the term *latency*. _____

Latency is the time between (the presentation of) a stimulus and (the occurrence of) a response. (or equivalent answer)

– –

11

Two things are *directly related* when an increase in one brings about an increase in the other.

Increasing heat causes the mercury in a thermometer to rise. Therefore, heat and the movement of mercury may be said to be _____
_____.

directly related

- -

12

In a reflex, as the intensity of the stimulus is increased, the magnitude of the response is (□ increased   □ decreased).

increased

- -

13

Therefore, stimulus intensity and response magnitude are _____ related.

directly

- -

14

If stimulus intensity is decreased, the magnitude of the response will _____.

decrease

- -

15

There is a direct relationship between the _____ of a response and the _____ of the stimulus.

magnitude   intensity

- -

16

When two things are directly related, an increase in one is accompanied by a(n) _____ in the other. Conversely, a decrease in one is accompanied by a(n) _____ in the other.

increase

decrease

- -

17

The intensity of a stimulus and the magnitude of the response are _____ related.

directly

- -

18

Let's take a different situation.

If you lost weight by exercising, then as you increased the amount of exercise you did, your weight would ⎯⎯⎯⎯⎯⎯.

decrease

- - - - - - - - - - - - - - - - - - - -

19

The opposite of a direct relationship is an *inverse relationship*. In an *inverse* relationship, an increase in one thing would be accompanied by a(n) (□ increase □ decrease) in the other.

decrease

- - - - - - - - - - - - - - - - - - - -

20

In the previous example, your weight and the amount of exercise you did would be (□ directly □ inversely) related.

inversely

- - - - - - - - - - - - - - - - - - - -

21

Latency is inversely related to the stimulus intensity. Therefore, as the intensity of a stimulus is increased, the latency of the response will:

□ increase
□ decrease

decrease

- - - - - - - - - - - - - - - - - - - -

22

A weak stimulus elicits a response with a long ⎯⎯⎯⎯⎯⎯. Therefore, response latency and stimulus intensity are ⎯⎯⎯⎯⎯⎯ related.

latency
inversely (indirectly is
  wrong)

- - - - - - - - - - - - - - - - - - - -

23

A strong stimulus elicits a response with a (□ long □ short) latency.

short

- - - - - - - - - - - - - - - - - - - -

24

The intensity of the stimulus is inversely related to the _____ of the _____.

latency (of the) response

— —

25

(Refer to Panel R-3-1, Figure I.)

In Figure I, changing the stimulus intensity from 1 to 2 *units* changes the value of A (on the vertical axis) from 25 to _____ units.

75

— —

26

(Refer to Panel R-3-1, Figure I.)

In other words, the relationship between intensity and A is (□ direct   □ inverse).

direct

— —

27

(Refer to Panel R-3-1, Figure I.)

You can guess, therefore, that A stands for response _____.

LABEL the vertical axis correctly on the panel.

magnitude
A = Response Magnitude

— —

28

What do we mean when we say that the relationship between stimulus intensity and response magnitude is a direct one? _____

We mean that an increase in stimulus intensity produces an increase in response magnitude, and a decrease in stimulus intensity produces a decrease in response magnitude.
(or equivalent answer)

— —

29

(Refer to Panel R-3-1, Figure II.)

When stimulus intensity is 1, B is _____.

When stimulus intensity is 2, B is _____.

When stimulus intensity is 3, B is _____.

As stimulus intensity increases, what happens to B? _____

This relationship is (□ direct □ inverse).

B stands for response _____.

LABEL the vertical axis correctly.

	40
	20
	10
	B decreases.
	inverse
	latency
	B = Response Latency

- -

30

(Refer to Panel R-3-1, Figure II.)

A decrease in response latency from 40 to 20 units is brought about by an increase in stimulus intensity from _____ to _____ units.

1 (to) 2

- -

31

(Refer to Panel R-3-1, Figure II.)

Between stimulus intensity and response latency there is a(n) _____ relationship.

inverse

- -

32

(Refer to Panel R-3-1.)

We will now consider Figures I and II together. In both figures, stimulus intensity is plotted on the (□ horizontal axis □ vertical axis).

horizontal axis

- -

33

(Refer to Panel R-3-1.)

Latency and magnitude are both plotted on the (□ horizontal axis □ vertical axis).

Both of these terms refer to measures of the (□ stimulus □ response).

vertical axis

response

- -

34

(Refer to Panel R-3-1.)

When studying behavior, we often measure several things at once. Figures I and II report results from the same experiment. We have measured the stimulus in _____ (how many) way(s), and we have measured the response in _____ (how many) way(s).

1
2

_ _

35

(Refer to Panel R-3-1.)

SUMMARIZE the results of the experiment by completing the following table:

Stimulus Intensity	Response Magnitude	Response Latency	Response Magnitude	Response Latency
0	0	—	(0)	(—)
1	25	40	(25)	(40)
2			75	20
3			100	10

_ _

36

As stimulus intensity increases, what happens to response magnitude? _____

Response magnitude increases.

As stimulus intensity increases, what happens to the latency of the response? _____

Response latency becomes shorter (decreases).

_ _

37

Response magnitude varies (□ directly □ inversely) with stimulus intensity.

directly

_ _

38

Response latency varies (□ directly □ inversely) with stimulus intensity.

inversely

_ _

39

Suppose a stimulus elicits a response with a long latency. You might predict that the magnitude of that response will be relatively (☐ large ☐ small).

small

40

(Refer to Panel R-3-1, Figure I.)

In Figure I, does a stimulus below 0.5 unit of intensity elicit a response?

    ☐ yes

    ☐ no

no

41

(Refer to Panel R-3-1, Figure I.)

Responses are elicited by stimuli above _____ unit(s) of intensity.

0.5

42

(Refer to Panel R-3-1, Figure I.)

What is the threshold value of the stimulus in the reflex we are studying?

_____ units(s) of _____

0.5 (unit of) stimulus intensity

43

(Refer to Panel R-3-1.)

CHECK the correct boxes:

Stimulus Intensity	Subliminal	Supraliminal
0.05	☐	☐
0.25	☐	☐
0.45	☐	☐
0.65	☐	☐
0.85	☐	☐

Subliminal	Supraliminal
☒	☐
☒	☐
☒	☐
☐	☒
☐	☒

44

Stimulus intensity is plotted on the (☐ horizontal ☐ vertical) axis of a graph.

Response magnitude and response latency are plotted on the (☐ horizontal ☐ vertical) axis of a graph.

horizontal

vertical

_____

45

In general, measures of the response are plotted on the _____ axis, while measures of the stimulus are plotted on the _____ axis.

vertical
horizontal

_____

46

As stimulus intensity increases, response magnitude (☐ increases ☐ decreases).

As stimulus intensity decreases, the latency (☐ increases ☐ decreases).

increases

increases

_____

47

The relationship between stimulus intensity and response magnitude is _____.

The relationship between stimulus intensity and response latency is _____.

direct

inverse

_____

48

Assume that we present a stimulus and no response occurs.

What is the value of the response magnitude?

_____

0

This stimulus would be (□ above □ below) threshold.

below

It would therefore be termed:
□ subliminal
□ supraliminal

subliminal

Could we measure a latency in this case?
□ yes
□ no

no

_ _

Stimulus-Response Relationships

1

In an experiment, a psychologist increases the intensity of a light, then measures the change in pupillary response. Which event occurs first?

☐ light intensity is increased

☐ pupil contraction is measured

light intensity is increased

- -

2

A psychologist measures the latency of a response at one stimulus intensity. Then he decreases the intensity of the stimulus and again measures response latency.

In the second case, the latency is likely to be:

☐ longer

☐ shorter

longer

Which does the psychologist change directly?

☐ stimulus intensity

☐ response latency

stimulus intensity

Which changes as a result?

☐ stimulus intensity

☐ response latency

response latency

- -

3

A subject's heart rate may increase when the experimenter "turns up" the shock. Which sentence describes the situation best?

☐ The heart rate depends on the shock.

☐ The shock intensity depends on the heart rate.

The heart rate depends on the shock.

- -

4

The name *independent variable* is given to the factor that the experimenter changes directly. The name *dependent variable* is given to the resulting changes that depend upon what was done.

If we study the way in which the concentration of lemon juice on the tongue affects the amount of saliva secreted by a dog, the independent variable is:

☐ amount of salivation
☐ concentration of lemon juice

The dependent variable is:

☐ amount of salivation
☐ concentration of lemon juice

concentration of lemon juice
amount of salivation

- -

5

If we study the effect of the size of print used in a book upon the speed at which the book can be read, print size is the (☐ dependent ☐ independent) variable and reading speed is the (☐ dependent ☐ independent) variable.

independent
dependent

- -

6

The response of a subject depends upon the stimulus. The experimenter can present and vary the stimulus as he pleases. The stimulus is the _____ variable, and the dependent variable is the _____.

independent
response

- -

7

Response magnitude and response latency are measures of the behavior of the subject that we are investigating. They are both _____ variables.

To change these behaviors, the experimenter must change stimulus intensity. Stimulus intensity is a(n):

    ☐ dependent variable
    ☐ independent variable

dependent

independent variable

- -

8

Here is the title of a psychological study: "The effect of Vitamin A dosage on accuracy of night vision."

The independent variable is:

    ☐ accuracy of night vision
    ☐ Vitamin A dosage

The dependent variable is:

    ☐ accuracy of night vision
    ☐ Vitamin A dosage

Vitamin A dosage

accuracy of night vision

- -

9

The experimenter manipulates the (☐ dependent ☐ independent) variable and notes the resulting changes in the (☐ dependent ☐ independent) variable.

independent
dependent

- -

10

The independent variable in psychology usually refers to (☐ a change in the environment ☐ the behavior of the subject).

The dependent variable refers to (☐ a change in the environment ☐ the behavior of the subject).

a change in the environment

the behavior of the subject

- -

11

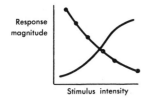

In this figure, the dependent variable is plotted along the (☐ horizontal ☐ vertical) axis and the independent variable is plotted along the (☐ horizontal ☐ vertical) axis.

vertical

horizontal

—————————————————————————

12

Here is another figure you have seen before:

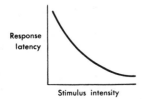

In this figure, the dependent variable is plotted along the (☐ horizontal ☐ vertical) axis and the independent variable is plotted along the (☐ horizontal ☐ vertical) axis.

vertical

horizontal

—————————————————————————

13

Often when we graph the results of a study, what variable do we plot on the vertical axis? _____

_____

dependent variable

What variable do we plot on the horizontal axis?

_____ _____

independent variable

—————————————————————————

14

An experiment is performed to study the time taken to eat a sandwich as a function of previous hours without food.

"Time to eat a sandwich" is the:

☐ dependent variable

☐ independent variable

"Previous hours without food" is the:

☐ dependent variable

☐ independent variable

Using the two phrases above, LABEL the axes of the figure below appropriately for presenting the results of the study:

- -

dependent variable

independent variable

Time to eat a sandwich

Previous hours without food

15

In this figure:

Response magnitude

Stimulus intensity

The dependent variable is _____ _____ and the independent variable is _____ _____.

- -

response magnitude
stimulus intensity

16

In this figure:

Response
latency

Stimulus intensity

The dependent variable is _____ _____
and the independent variable is _____

_____.

response latency
stimulus intensity

- -

17

Suppose that a study investigated *number of drops of saliva* as a function of *concentration of lemon juice* on the tongue. The independent variable would be _____.
The dependent variable would be _____.

concentration of lemon juice
number of drops of saliva

- -

18

LABEL the two axes of the graph appropriately for this study of the *number of drops of saliva* as a function of the *concentration of lemon juice:*

Number of
drops of
saliva

Concentration
of lemon juice

- -

19

A graph is a quick and pictorial way of representing some types of data. We often also use symbols as shorthand. The symbol S stands for stimulus. Obviously, the symbol for response is _____.

R

- -

20

S = _____   stimulus
R = _____   response

- -

21

A reflex is defined as the elicitation of a(n)
_____ by a(n) _____   response *or* R
                                             stimulus *or* S

- -

22

In this notation:

$$S \longrightarrow R$$

the arrow from S to R is read *elicits*.
WRITE the expression above (S ————►R)
as a complete English sentence. _____   A stimulus elicits a re-
                                                        sponse.

- -

23

The notation:

$$S \longrightarrow R$$

denotes the elicitation of a response by a stimulus.
It is therefore the notation of a(n) _____.   reflex

- -

24

Instead of writing out the definition of a reflex,
we can indicate it by the symbolic notation:
_____ $$S \longrightarrow R$$

- -

25

The symbolic notation for a relation is called a
paradigm (pronounced "para-dim" or "para-dime").
The symbols:

$$S \longrightarrow R$$

are a(n) _____ for a(n) _____.   paradigm   reflex

- -

26

A stimulus elicits a response.
WRITE the paradigm for the sentence above.

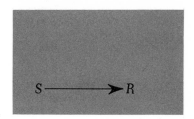

_____

The Principle of Reflex Conditioning (Pavlovian Conditioning)

1

In a hungry dog, we can demonstrate the following reflex: *Food in mouth elicits salivation.*

In the paradigm below, FILL IN the parentheses with the names of the stimulus and the response for this reflex:

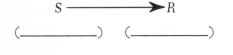

S ————————➤ R

(_____)   (_____)

- -

2

    Light in eye elicits pupil contraction.

COMPLETE the paradigm for the reflex above (two letters are required):

_____   _____

(light   (pupil
in eye)   contraction)

- -

3

    Electric shock applied to the hand elicits increased heart rate.

DRAW and LABEL the complete paradigm for the reflex above:

- -

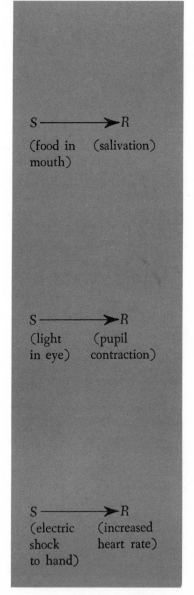

S ————————➤ R
(food in   (salivation)
mouth)

S ————————➤ R
(light   (pupil
in eye)   contraction)

S ————————➤ R
(electric   (increased
shock   heart rate)
to hand)

4

Some stimuli elicit responses without previous learning. DRAW lines from the stimuli to the responses which they elicit:

Stimuli	*Responses*
food	pupil contraction
light	increased heart rate
electric shock	salivation

food — pupil contraction
light — increased heart rate
electric — salivation
shock

- -

5

A stimulus that elicits a response without previous training is called an *unconditioned stimulus.*

Which do you think is an unconditioned stimulus for the response of salivation?

☐ food in the mouth

☐ a menu

food in the mouth

- -

6

Other stimuli acquire their power to elicit responses only through training or learning. These are called *conditioned stimuli.*

Which do you think might be a conditioned stimulus for increased heart rate?

☐ the sound of a nearby explosion (dynamite)

☐ the sight of the burning fuse

the sight of the burning fuse

- -

7

A light in the eye is an unconditioned _____ for pupil contraction.

stimulus

- -

8

The sound of a dentist's drill might be a(n) _____ stimulus for nausea and trembling.

conditioned

- -

9

For a Frenchman, a French menu might be a conditioned _____ for a salivary response.

stimulus

- -

10

A stimulus that elicits a response without prior training is called a(n) _____ stimulus.

unconditioned

- -

11

A reflex prompted by an unconditioned stimulus is called a(n) _____ reflex.

unconditioned

- -

12

$S \longrightarrow R$ is the paradigm for any _____.

reflex

- -

13

If S stands for stimulus, then you might guess that the notation for an Unconditioned Stimulus would be _____.

US

- -

14

In the paradigm:

$$US \longrightarrow R$$

the symbol US stands for _____ _____.
The arrow stands for the word _____.
The R stands for _____.

unconditioned stimulus
elicits
response

- -

15

The paradigm:

$$US \longrightarrow R$$

designates a(n) _____ reflex.

unconditioned

- -

16

The paradigm for an unconditioned reflex is

____ ____ ____

$$US \longrightarrow R$$

17

In this paradigm:

$$US \longrightarrow R$$

the arrow signifies the word _____.

elicits

18

An unconditioned stimulus is one that will elicit a response without _____.

previous training or learning
(or equivalent answer)

19

On the other hand, the ability of some stimuli to elicit responses is conditional (depends) upon some kind of prior training. We have called such stimuli _____ed stimuli.

conditioned

20

Stimuli that elicit responses without previous training are called:
- ☐ conditioned stimuli
- ☐ unconditioned stimuli

unconditioned stimuli

21

$$US \longrightarrow R$$

Which reflex is an appropriate instance of the paradigm above?
- ☐ photograph elicits blushing
- ☐ rotten food elicits vomiting

rotten food elicits vomiting

22

Suppose that we present a puppy with an empty food dish. It is the first time he has ever seen the dish. He looks at the dish. We notice that he does not salivate. Is the dish a *US* for salivation?

☐ yes

☐ no

no

- -

23

The stimulus (empty food dish) does not elicit the response without training. In this respect it is initially a:

☐ neutral stimulus

☐ powerful stimulus

neutral stimulus

- -

24

We know that food in the mouth will produce salivation without previous training. Food in the mouth acts as the _____ stimulus, which is abbreviated _____.

unconditioned

US

- -

25

Suppose that we put food in the dish. The puppy looks at the dish and then eats the food.

The dish is a stimulus, and so is the food in the mouth. Which stimulus comes first in time?

☐ the dish

☐ food in the mouth

the dish

- -

26

After feeding the puppy from the dish a number of times, we notice that when we now put the food dish in front of the puppy he salivates. The dish was once a neutral stimulus. Is it now?

☐ yes

☐ no

no

- -

27

FILL IN the terms in the unconditioned reflex just described:

$$US \longrightarrow R$$

(_____) (_____)

What is the neutral stimulus we are pairing with the *US*? _____

$US \longrightarrow R$
(food in (salivation) the mouth)
the dish

- -

28

The food dish was once a neutral stimulus. But after it has been paired with the *US* of _____ a number of times, it has acquired the power to elicit a similar _____.

food *or* sight of food

response

- -

29

The food dish was a neutral stimulus. We paired it repeatedly with a *US* for the response of _____.

salivating *or* salivation

- -

30

A reflex whose stimulus is a conditioned stimulus is called a *conditioned reflex*. In the conditioned reflex we have just formed in the puppy, the conditioned stimulus is _____ and the response is _____.

the dish *or* sight of dish salivation

- -

31

Food in the mouth elicits salivation is a(n):
- ☐ conditioned reflex
- ☐ unconditioned reflex

Sight of dish elicits salivation is a(n):
- ☐ conditioned reflex
- ☐ unconditioned reflex

unconditioned reflex

conditioned reflex

- -

32

The "rule" for producing a conditioned reflex is simple: A previously neutral stimulus is paired with a(n) _____ stimulus. The neutral stimulus then becomes a(n) _____ stimulus.

unconditioned
conditioned

33

If the abbreviation for *unconditioned stimulus* is *US,* you would guess that we abbreviate conditioned stimulus as _____.

CS

34

NUMBER these events in the proper order:

    a. _____ The conditioned stimulus elicits a response.

    b. _____ The neutral stimulus does not elicit a response.

    c. _____ The neutral stimulus is paired with a *US.*

Which of the three statements above describes the *procedure* for producing a conditioned reflex?
_____

a. 3

b. 1

c. 2

c.

35

The *CS* must precede or simultaneously accompany the presentation of the *US.* Therefore, if we were to present the food first and then the food dish, we (☐ would ☐ would not) produce a conditioned reflex.

would not

36

For successful conditioning, the *CS* must:

    ☐ precede or accompany the *US*

    ☐ follow the *US*

precede or accompany the *US*

37

The procedure for producing a conditioned reflex is called *conditioning*.

Conditioning takes place when we pair a neutral stimulus with a(n) _____ _____.

The neutral stimulus then becomes a(n)_____ _____.

unconditioned stimulus *or US*

conditioned stimulus *or CS*

- -

38

If a CS and US are not presented simultaneously, which must come first if conditioning is to take place?

- [ ] CS
- [ ] US

CS

- -

39

CS ⟶ R

How would you read the paradigm above? _____

A conditioned stimulus elicits a response. (You could also have said "conditioned reflex.")

- -

40

We know that a procedure called conditioning has taken place when a formerly neutral stimulus now _____ the response when presented by itself.

elicits

- -

41

The name of the procedure used when we pair a neutral stimulus with a US so that the neutral stimulus becomes a CS is _____.

conditioning

- -

42

DESCRIBE in words the procedure for producing a conditioned reflex. ⸺⸺⸺

A neutral stimulus is paired with an unconditioned stimulus (or *US*) and becomes a conditioned stimulus (or *CS*). (or equivalent answer)

Forming Conditioned Reflexes

1

Suppose we take a stimulus that initially has no effect (is neutral). After it has been paired with an unconditioned stimulus, the previously neutral stimulus will now be a(n) _____.

conditioned stimulus

- -

2

MATCH the following with connecting lines:

the *procedure* □   □ An originally neutral
of conditioning   stimulus is paired with
     an unconditioned stimu-
     lus.

□————□

the *result* of □   □ The neutral stimulus
the procedure   becomes able to elicit
     a response.

□————□

- -

3

We can say that there is a conditioned reflex when a previously neutral stimulus _____ a response similar to the one the *US* elicits.

elicits

- -

4

In our descriptions, the term "neutral" refers to the same physical stimulus as the term:

    □ CS
    □ US

CS

Before conditioning, we call it a:

    □ CS
    □ neutral stimulus

neutral stimulus

After conditioning, we call it a:

    □ CS
    □ neutral stimulus

CS

- -

5

The sound of a buzzer does not initially produce pupil contraction. The buzzer is an example of a(n):

☐ conditioned stimulus
☐ neutral stimulus
☐ unconditioned stimulus

neutral stimulus

- -

6

A flash of light (stimulus) automatically (without prior training) produces pupil contraction (response). The relationship:

$$US \longrightarrow R$$

(flash of light)   (pupil contraction)

is therefore a(n) _____ _____ .

unconditioned reflex

- -

7

To make the sound of a buzzer part of a conditioned reflex involving pupil contraction, we could:

☐ precede it with a flash of light
☐ follow it with a flash of light

follow it with a flash of light

- -

8

Before conditioning, the buzzer is a(n) _____ stimulus.

neutral

- -

9

The formation of a reflex relation between the buzzer and pupil contraction occurs through the procedure technically known as _____ .

conditioning

- -

10

In any reflex, a _____ _____ a _____ .

stimulus elicits response

- -

11

There are two kinds of reflexes: unconditioned and conditioned. When a *US* elicits a response, which kind is it? _____ _____

unconditioned reflex

12

And when a *CS* elicits a response, we have a(n) _____ _____.

conditioned reflex

13

$$US \longrightarrow R \qquad CS \longrightarrow R$$
$$\quad\;\; \textcircled{A} \qquad\qquad\quad\;\; \textcircled{B}$$

Light in eye elicits pupil contraction.
This is a(n) _____ reflex and is best illustrated by (☐ paradigm *A*   ☐ paradigm *B*).

unconditioned
paradigm *A*

Sight of food dish elicits salivation.
This is a(n) _____ reflex and is best illustrated by (☐ paradigm *A*   ☐ paradigm *B*).

conditioned
paradigm *B*

14

Remember: In order to have any reflex we must have both a(n) _____ and a(n) _____.

stimulus   response

15

In order to build a conditioned reflex, we start off with a stimulus that does not elicit the response and is therefore _____. This stimulus will become the _____ stimulus.

neutral
conditioned

16

We combine or pair the neutral stimulus with a(n) _____ stimulus.

unconditioned

17

When we combine two objects, we have a *pair*.
When we combine a neutral S with a *US,* we can speak of _____ the two stimuli.

pairing

— —

18

The procedure of pairing the neutral stimulus and the *US* causes the neutral stimulus to become a _____.

CS *or* conditioned stimulus

— —

19

When the CS elicits a response, this relationship is known as a _____ _____.

conditioned reflex

— —

20

Let's review. We know that food in the mouth elicits salivation.

The relationship:

$$S \longrightarrow R$$

 (food)   (salivation)

is a(n) _____ reflex.

unconditioned

— —

21

Initially the sight of the food dish does not elicit salivation. Therefore, prior to training, the sight of the food dish is a(n) _____ stimulus.

neutral

— —

22

If we want to make the sight of the food dish elicit salivation, we pair the sight of the food dish with _____.

food (in the mouth)

— —

23

After doing so, we find that the sight of the food dish _____ salivation.

elicits

— —

24

We have produced a(n) _____ reflex.
The CS for this reflex is _____.

conditioned
sight of the food dish

- -

25

A new conditioned reflex is like the original unconditioned reflex, except that one important part
has changed. Which statement describes that
change?

 ☐ A similar response is now elicited by a
  different stimulus.

 ☐ A different response is now elicited by the
  same stimulus.

A similar response is now
elicited by a different
stimulus.

- -

26

Stimulus substitution has taken place.
A(n):

 ☐ conditioned stimulus
 ☐ unconditioned stimulus

has been substituted for a(n):

 ☐ conditioned stimulus
 ☐ unconditioned stimulus

conditioned stimulus

unconditioned stimulus

- -

Number of Pairings as an Independent Variable

1

Suppose you owned a puppy. There are many sounds and sights that would accompany his daily feedings (footsteps, cans rattling, getting food dish off floor, etc.). Each of these stimuli would, in time, elicit salivation. These stimuli would play the role of CS in a _____ _____.

conditioned reflex

- -

2

These sounds and sights would become CS's through pairing with the US of _____. This pairing procedure is called _____.

food
conditioning

- -

3

The conditioning procedure depends upon the _____ of two stimuli.

pairing

- -

4

$US \longrightarrow R$ is the paradigm for a(n) _____ reflex.

unconditioned

- -

5

$US \longrightarrow R$ is the paradigm for condition-
$CS \dashrightarrow$ ing a new reflex.

US stands for the _____.

The arrow is read _____.

CS stands for the _____ _____.

The new reflex is indicated by the dashed line connecting _____ and _____.

unconditioned stimulus
elicits
conditioned stimulus

CS (and) R

- -

6

In the paradigm: $US \longrightarrow R$

  $CS \dashrightarrow$

the pairing is between the _____ and the _____.

_____

7

$US \longrightarrow R$

$CS \dashrightarrow$

The fact that the CS is written under the US suggests that the two stimuli are presented at about the same _____.

_____

8

In the paradigm: $US \longrightarrow R$

  $CS \dashrightarrow$

the dashed diagonal line (_ _ _) means that the CS is acquiring the power to elicit the _____.

_____

9

DRAW and LABEL with appropriate symbols the paradigm for establishing a conditioned reflex.

_____

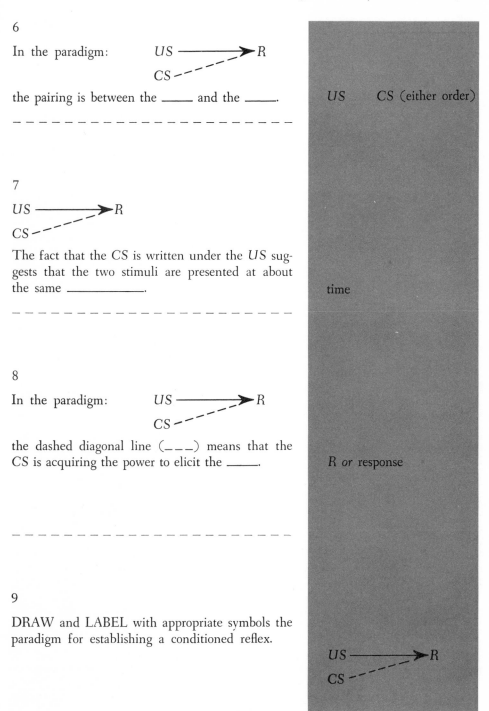

US   CS (either order)

time

R *or* response

$US \longrightarrow R$

$CS \dashrightarrow$

10

If a puppy salivates upon seeing an empty food dish, the conditioning procedure could be shown as:

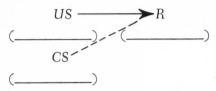

US = food in mouth
CS = empty food dish

R = salivation

11

Once the CS elicits the response, we have a _____ reflex.

conditioned

12

DRAW a paradigm for the conditioned reflex by showing the conditioned stimulus eliciting the response. The line which was dashed in the diagram of the procedure should now be solid, since the new reflex is formed; it should be horizontal instead of diagonal; and since it is now eliciting the response, an arrow should be added.

CS ——————➤R

13

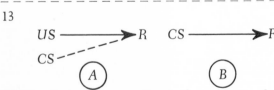

Which of the two paradigms above shows the pairing procedure? _____

A

Shows a conditioned reflex after conditioning is complete? _____

B

Incorporates an unconditioned reflex? _____

A

Must be carried out before the other paradigm can be attained? _____

A

Shows a "new" stimulus eliciting an "old" response? _____

B

14

A college student proposed to demonstrate conditioning by learning to control his own heart rate. The procedure he devised involved pairing a pistol shot with the spoken word *palpitate*. The pistol shot initially produced a rapid heart rate, and therefore was the _____.

unconditioned stimulus *or US*

- - - - - - - - - - - - - - - - - - -

15

The word *palpitate* does not normally cause increased heart rate. It is therefore a neutral stimulus, which the student hoped to turn into a(n) _____.

conditioned stimulus *or* CS

- - - - - - - - - - - - - - - - - - -

16

Now, if the word *palpitate* is said just before a pistol shot, we are pairing the two. COMPLETE the paradigm below:

$$US \longrightarrow R$$
(shot)   (rapid
heart rate)

____ ____
(_____)

CS
(palpitate)

- - - - - - - - - - - - - - - - - - -

17

With repeated pairing, the word *palpitate* alone will _____ rapid heart rate.

DRAW and LABEL a paradigm for the completed conditioned reflex.

elicit

$$CS \longrightarrow R$$
(palpitate) (rapid heart
rate)

- - - - - - - - - - - - - - - - - - -

18

(Look at Panel R-7-1.)

Let us now examine some laboratory studies that illustrate precise control and accurate observation of the conditioning process.

(READ THROUGH PANEL R-7-1. You will refer to this panel for frames 19 through 42.)

Pavlov's experiment was concerned with the conditioning of the _____ reflex.

The organism used as an experimental subject was a _____.

salivary

dog

- -

19

(Refer to Panel R-7-1.)

In this experiment, identify the:

      1. R _____

      2. CS _____

      3. US _____

1. salivation *or* drops of saliva
   (or equivalent answer)
2. sound of the metronome
3. food in the dog's mouth

- -

20

(Refer to Panel R-7-1.)

Session I demonstrated the:

    □ conditioned reflex
    □ unconditioned reflex

unconditioned reflex

- -

21

(Refer to Panel R-7-1.)

DRAW and LABEL the paradigm for the unconditioned reflex in Pavlov's experiment.

US ⟶ R
(food in   (salivation)
mouth)

- -

22

(Refer to Panel R-7-1.)

What was the latency of the salivation response to the food stimulus? _____

2 seconds

- -

23

(Refer to Panel R-7-1.)

Are *US* and *CS* paired in Session II?

☐ yes

☐ no

no

- -

24

(Refer to Panel R-7-1.)

What could you do to demonstrate that the metronome was originally a neutral stimulus? _____

present the metronome without the food

Did Pavlov do this? ☐ yes ☐ no

yes

Did the response occur? ☐ yes ☐ no

no

- -

25

(Refer to Panel R-7-1.)

In which session did the actual conditioning take place? _____

Session III

- -

26

(Refer to Panel R-7-1.)

What are the two stimuli that are paired in Session III? (NAME the specific stimuli.)

_____

_____

food in mouth
sound of metronome
(either order)

- -

27

(Refer to Panel R-7-1.)

What time interval elapsed between presentation of the CS and the US? _____

5 seconds

- -

28

(Refer to Panel R-7-1.)

DRAW the paradigm for the first trial of Session III. Again, LABEL the actual experimental stimuli and response. (*Don't forget the dotted line!*)

US ⟶ R
(food in   (salivation)
mouth)
  CS
(sound of
metronome)

- -

29

(Refer to Panel R-7-1.)

How many times were CS and US paired in Pavlov's experiment? _____

10 times

- -

30

(Refer to Panel R-7-1.)

Each pairing in the experiment is called a *trial*. Measures of the conditioned reflex were obtained at Trial No. _____ and Trial No. _____.

5   10

- -

31

(Refer to Panel R-7-1.)

How would you draw the paradigm of the new reflex that has been established? LABEL the actual stimulus and response.

CS ⟶ R
(sound of   (salivation)
metronome)

- -

32

(Refer to Panel R-7-1.)

The metronome in Session II was shown to be a neutral stimulus because when it was sounded _____.

In Session III, the neutral stimulus became a _____.

no salivation occurred (or equivalent answer)

CS

--- --- --- --- --- --- --- --- --- --- --- --- --- --- ---

33

(Refer to Panel R-7-1.)

Pavlov used two measures of the response that we have seen before: latency and magnitude.

Latency was measured in:
  □ drops of saliva
  □ seconds

Magnitude was measured in:
  □ drops of saliva
  □ seconds

seconds

drops of saliva

--- --- --- --- --- --- --- --- --- --- --- --- --- --- ---

34

(Refer to Panel R-7-1.)

The latency, to be more precise, was the time, in seconds, from the beginning of a stimulus to the beginning of a(n) _____.

R (salivation)

--- --- --- --- --- --- --- --- --- --- --- --- --- --- ---

35

(Refer to Panel R-7-1.)

Let us examine changes in the magnitude of the response.

In Session I, the *US* was presented alone, and response magnitude was _____ drops of saliva.

15

In Session II, before any pairings, the metronome was a neutral stimulus, and elicited _____ drops.

0

In Session III, after five pairings of metronome and food, the *CS* elicited _____ drops.

3

After ten pairings, the CS elicited _____ drops.

10

36

(Refer to Panel R-7-1.)

$$US \longrightarrow R$$
(food) $\quad$ (salivation)

$$CS$$
(metronome)

Repeated pairings in the conditioning procedure above have the following effect upon the conditioned reflex:

What happens to the magnitude of the response to the *CS*? _____

It increases *or* gets larger.

37

(Refer to Panel R-7-1.)

Now let us examine changes in the latency.

In Session I, the *US* was presented alone, and response latency was _____ seconds.

2

In Session II, the metronome elicited no response. Could a latency be measured?

☐ yes

☐ no

no

In Session III, after five pairings of metronome and food, the latency to the *CS* was _____ seconds.

4

After ten pairings, the latency was _____ seconds.

2

38

(Refer to Panel R-7-1.)

$$US \longrightarrow R$$
(food)   (salivation)

CS

(metronome)

What effect do repeated pairings in the conditioning procedure have upon the latency of the response to the CS? _____

The latency decreases *or* gets smaller.

_____

39

(Refer to Panel R-7-1.)

The procedure for conditioning consists in pairings of a _____ with a _____.

CS   US
(either order)

The result of this procedure is a new reflex:

$$CS \longrightarrow R$$

The results of repeated pairings upon this new reflex are that:

Response magnitude _____.

Latency _____.

increases *or* gets larger
decreases *or* gets smaller

_____

40

(Refer to Panel R-7-1.)

You will remember that response latency and response magnitude are both examples of:

☐ dependent variables

☐ independent variables

dependent variables

_____

41 (Refer to Panel R-7-1.)

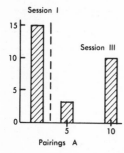
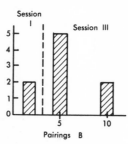

Graph *A* shows the changes in one dependent variable measured by Pavlov. Which one is it?

_____

The values on the vertical axis represent _____.

Graph *B* shows the changes in the second dependent variable measured by Pavlov. Which one is it? _____

The values on the vertical axis represent _____.

— —

42

Latency and magnitude are both dependent variables that describe aspects of:

☐ responses, or parts of behavior

☐ stimuli, or parts of the environment

— —

43

As conditioning progresses, these variables change. To test the new reflex, we present the _____ alone, and find that the _____ of the response increases, while its _____ decreases.

— —

magnitude

drops (of saliva)

latency

seconds (time in seconds)

responses, or parts of behavior

CS
magnitude
latency

44

When a dependent variable changes value, we look for the independent variable that accounts for the change. In Pavlov's experiment, was the intensity of the US changed?

☐ yes

☐ no

no

Was the intensity of the CS changed?

☐ yes

☐ no

no

Was the number of pairings of the CS and the US changed?

☐ yes

☐ no

yes

- -

45

The variable that the experimenter manipulates directly is the:

☐ dependent variable

☐ independent variable

independent variable

In Pavlov's experiment, the experimenter directly manipulated:

☐ latency and magnitude

☐ the number of pairings

the number of pairings

- -

46

The number of pairings of CS and US is a(n) _____ variable.

independent

The resulting change in response latency in the conditioned reflex is a(n) _____ variable.

dependent

The resulting change in response magnitude in the conditioned reflex is a(n) _____ variable.

dependent

- -

47

With an increased number of pairings, the latency of salivation:

☐ increases

☐ decreases

decreases

- -

48

Latency of salivation and number of stimulus pairings are:

☐ directly related

☐ inversely related

inversely related

Magnitude of salivation and number of stimulus pairings are:

☐ directly related

☐ inversely related

directly related

- -

49

(Look at Panel R-7-2.)

In Anrep's study, biscuit powder in the mouth was the _____.

US

The originally neutral stimulus, which became a CS when paired with the biscuit powder, was a _____.

tone (of 637.5 cycles per second)

- -

50

(Refer to Panel R-7-2.)

During conditioning, the CS lasted for _____ seconds.

5

The US was presented _____ seconds later.

2 or 3

Thus:

☐ the CS preceded the US

☐ the US preceded the CS

the CS preceded the US

- -

51

(Refer to Panel R-7-2.)

DRAW and LABEL a paradigm of the conditioning procedure in Anrep's experiment.

US ⟶ R
(biscuit (salivation)
powder)
CS
(tone)

- -

52

(Refer to Panel R-7-2.)

At irregular intervals of 5 to 35 minutes, the experimenter repeatedly _____ the CS with the US.

paired

- -

53

(Refer to Panel R-7-2.)

The experiment lasted 16 days, and over this period the total number of pairings was _____.

50

The progress of the conditioned reflex was tested by presenting the _____ alone.

CS *or* tone

This testing occurred _____ times.

6

- -

54

(Refer to Panel R-7-2.)

US ⟶ R   CS ⟶ R
CS
Ⓐ   Ⓑ

Which paradigm represents the pairing procedure, repeated 50 times? _____

A

Which paradigm represents the testing procedure, repeated 6 times? _____

B

- -

55

(Refer to Panel R-7-2.)

The dependent variables were:

_____ of the response, which was measured in _____ of _____; _____ of the response, which was measured in _____.

- -

56

(Refer to Panel R-7-2.)

Did one pairing establish a conditioned reflex in this experiment?

□ yes

□ no

After 30 pairings, response magnitude was _____ drops, and the latency was _____ seconds.

- -

57

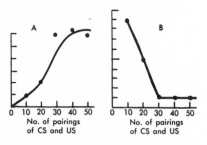

Graph *A* shows the effects of conditioning upon the _____ of the response.

Graph *B* shows the effects of conditioning upon the _____ of the response.

- -

58

MATCH the following:

a. the scientist who first studied conditioned reflexes

b. the favorite subject used in studies of conditioned reflexes

c. the response often used in studies of conditioned reflexes

1. ____dog

2. ____Ivan Pavlov

3. ____salivation

1. *b.*

2. *a.*

3. *c.*

- -

59

The kind of conditioning described in this section has come to be named for the man who first studied it. Hence it is known as Pavlovian conditioning. Every case of Pavlovian conditioning involves at least _____ (how many) stimuli.

2

- -

60

DRAW and LABEL the paradigm for the unconditioned reflex used by Pavlov and Anrep.

US ————————➤ R
(food)   (salivation)

- -

61

The formation of a new conditioned reflex is the result of _____ conditioning.

This is accomplished by the _____ of a CS and a US.

Typically, the ____ precedes the ____ by a few seconds.

Pavlovian

pairing

CS   US

- -

62

The result of such pairings is that the CS comes to _____ the R.

As the new reflex gets stronger:

    response magnitude _____;

    response latency _____.

elicit

increases *or* gets larger
decreases *or* gets shorter

- -

63

In Pavlovian conditioning, large magnitudes and short latencies are produced by:

    ☐ few pairings of CS and US

    ☐ many pairings of CS and US

many pairings of CS and US

- -

64

SKETCH the general trend in the magnitude and the latency as repeated pairings of CS and US established a conditioned reflex:

Magnitude   No. of pairings

Latency   No. of pairings

- -

65

In Pavlovian conditioning, magnitude and latency are commonly used (☐ dependent ☐ independent) variables.

dependent

- -

66

The independent variable in Anrep's experiment was _____.

the number of pairings (of CS and US)

- -

Temporal Patterns in Conditioning

1

PREVIEW FRAME

Any given stimulus may last a short time or a long time. When two stimuli are paired, as in conditioning, the time relations between them may affect the conditioning process. This set will take up these questions in some detail.

NO RESPONSE REQUIRED

NO RESPONSE REQUIRED; GO ON TO NEXT FRAME.

2

The diagram above represents the presentation of a single stimulus. The horizontal line jogs upward with the _____ of the stimulus, and back down again with its _____.

onset
termination

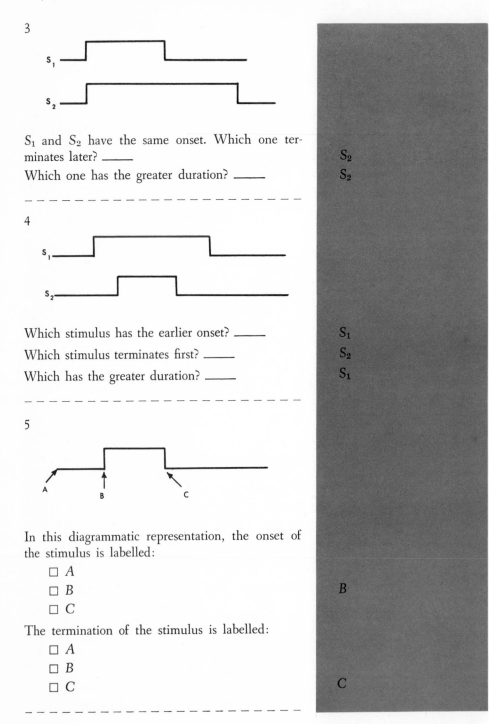

3

S_1 and S_2 have the same onset. Which one terminates later? ——

Which one has the greater duration? ——

S_2

S_2

- -

4

Which stimulus has the earlier onset? ——

Which stimulus terminates first? ——

Which has the greater duration? ——

S_1

S_2

S_1

- -

5

In this diagrammatic representation, the onset of the stimulus is labelled:

☐ A

☐ B

☐ C

The termination of the stimulus is labelled:

☐ A

☐ B

☐ C

B

C

- -

6

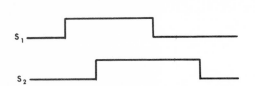

Here are two stimuli. Each has an onset and a termination. COMPLETE the list of the four events in the temporal order shown in the diagram:

First: the onset of S_1.

Second: the _____ of _____.

Third: the _____ of _____.

Fourth: the _____ of _____.

(First: the onset of S_1.)

Second: the onset of S_2

Third: the termination of S_1.

Fourth: the termination of S_2.

- -

7

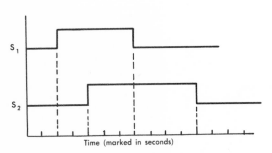

Time (marked in seconds)

The duration of S_1 is ____ seconds.

The onset of S_2 follows the onset of S_1 by ____ seconds.

Thus, the two stimuli *overlap* during the last ____ seconds of S_1.

What is the duration of S_2? ____ seconds.

How long does S_2 persist after S_1 is terminated? ____ seconds.

Thus, the two stimuli overlap during the first ____ seconds of S_2.

5

2

3

7

4

3

8

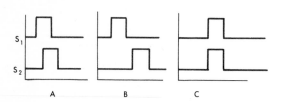

S_1 and S_2 are two stimuli of equal duration. In the blank following each descriptive sentence below, WRITE the letter of the diagram that the sentence describes:

The amount of overlap between S_1 and S_2 is greatest when their onsets and terminations are simultaneous. _____   *C*

There is some overlap when the onset of S_1 precedes the onset of S_2, but the onset of S_2 precedes the termination of S_1. _____   *A*

There is no overlap when the termination of S_1 precedes the onset of S_2. _____   *B*

- -

9

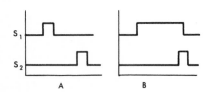

Which case—*A* or *B*—most closely resembles the time relations when:

    the smell of food precedes tasting it? _____   *B*

    the cocking of a pistol precedes the noise of its firing? _____   *A*

    a flash of distant lightning precedes the sound of thunder? _____   *A*

    the whine of an artillery shell precedes the sound of its explosion? _____   *B*

- -

10

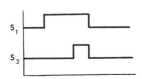

The relation between any two stimuli can be diagrammed as we have been doing. But we are interested in cases in which one of the stimuli is an
unconditioned stimulus. The diagram above resembles the pairing procedure employed by Pavlov
and Anrep. Which stimulus in the picture is the
US? ____

S_2

– –

11

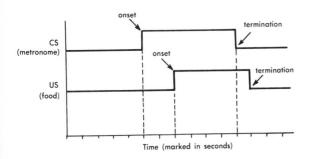

The figure above shows graphically a conditioning
procedure that is commonly employed.

The onset of the CS precedes the onset of the *US*
by ____ seconds.

The CS and the *US* overlap for ____ seconds.

2

4

– –

12

This procedure, in which the CS precedes the US by a short interval and the CS overlaps the US in time, is known as *simultaneous* conditioning.

Which of these two diagrams represents *simultaneous conditioning*? (CHECK ONE.)

A ☐   B ☐

B

- -

13

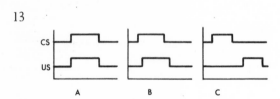

CS

US

A   B   C

A procedure for pairing CS and US is called *simultaneous*:

1. if the CS and the US begin at the same instant. This is the case in diagram _____.

    or

2. if the CS precedes the US only by a short interval. This is the case in diagram _____.

    and

3. whether the CS precedes the US or not, the two stimuli have some overlap in time. This is the case in both _____ and _____.

The one case above that is *not* an example of simultaneous pairing is _____.

A

B

A (and) *B*

C

- -

14

We call both of the procedures diagrammed above *simultaneous* even though the stimuli are *strictly* simultaneous only in the case of _____.

We have loosened our definition of simultaneous to include cases in which the CS precedes the US by a (□ long □ short) interval, and in which there is (□ some overlap □ no overlap) between the stimuli.

- -

15

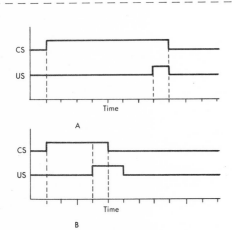

But what do we mean by "short"? We arbitrarily use a 5-second limit between the onset of the CS and that of the US to define simultaneous conditioning.

In case A above, the two onsets are separated by _____ seconds.

In case B, the two onsets are separated by _____ seconds.

Which case is an example of simultaneous conditioning? _____

- -

A

short
some overlap

7

3

B

16

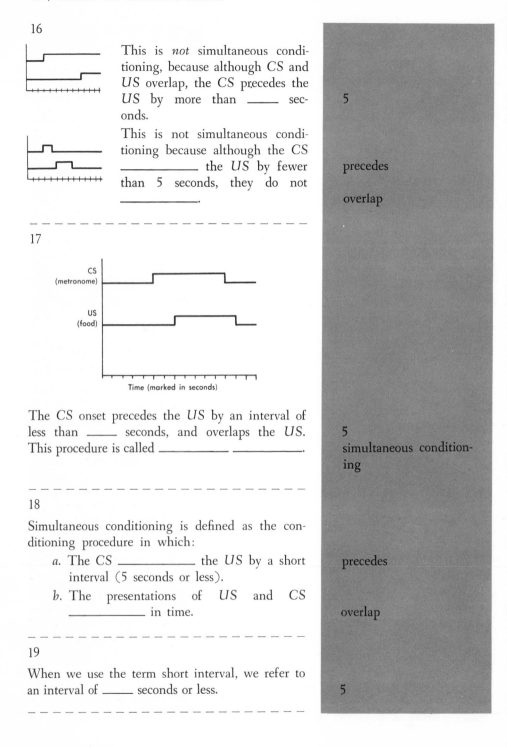

This is *not* simultaneous conditioning, because although CS and US overlap, the CS precedes the US by more than _____ seconds.

5

This is not simultaneous conditioning because although the CS _____ the US by fewer than 5 seconds, they do not _____.

precedes

overlap

- -

17

The CS onset precedes the US by an interval of less than _____ seconds, and overlaps the US. This procedure is called _____ _____.

5

simultaneous conditioning

- -

18

Simultaneous conditioning is defined as the conditioning procedure in which:

    a. The CS _____ the US by a short interval (5 seconds or less).

    b. The presentations of US and CS _____ in time.

precedes

overlap

- -

19

When we use the term short interval, we refer to an interval of _____ seconds or less.

5

- -

20

Simultaneous conditioning can be defined as a conditioning procedure in which:

    a. The CS _____ the *US* by 5 seconds or less.

    b. The CS and *US* _____.

precedes

overlap

- -

21

To test whether the conditioning procedure has been *successful,* we would present the CS alone and observe whether the _____ occurs.

response

- -

22

Pavlov and other workers have found simultaneous conditioning to be a powerful pairing procedure. This means that the formation of conditioned reflexes is (☐ difficult ☐ easy) when using this procedure.

easy

- -

23

They have also found conditioning to be most effective when the CS precedes the *US* by an interval of about one-fourth of a second to two seconds. Does this fall within the definition of simultaneous conditioning?

    ☐ yes

    ☐ no

Thus, if CS and *US* are *strictly* simultaneous, conditioning is (☐ less effective ☐ more effective) than when the CS precedes the *US* by a short interval.

yes

less effective

- -

24

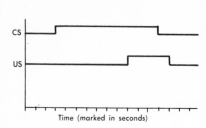

Time (marked in seconds)

LOOK at the diagrammed procedure above.
Does the CS overlap the US? ☐ yes ☐ no
Does the CS precede the US? ☐ yes ☐ no
If it does, by how many seconds? _____

yes
yes
7

_ _

25

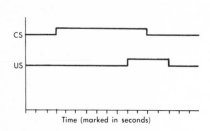

Time (marked in seconds)

In terms of our definition, does the CS precede
the US by a long interval or a short interval?

_____

by a long interval

_ _

26

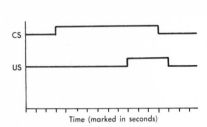

For simultaneous conditioning:

a. The CS must _____ the US by
   _____ seconds or less.

b. The CS and the US must _____
   in time.

Does the procedure illustrated in the diagram satisfy both of these criteria for simultaneous conditioning?

☐ yes ☐ no

CIRCLE the statement letter(s) above that the diagrammed procedure satisfies.

precede
5

overlap

no

You should have circled *b*.

— — — — — — — — — — — — — — — — — — — —

27

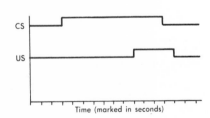

This diagram does not picture the procedure of simultaneous conditioning. Why not? _____

because the CS begins more than 5 seconds before the US
(or equivalent answer)

— — — — — — — — — — — — — — — — — — — —

28

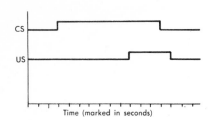

Time (marked in seconds)

This procedure is known as *delayed conditioning*. In what two ways is it like simultaneous conditioning?

a. _____

b. _____

a. The CS precedes the US.
b. The CS overlaps the US.

- -

29

Delayed conditioning is unlike simultaneous conditioning in that the CS precedes the US by
_____.

more than 5 seconds

- -

30

If the CS begins a "long" time before the US and overlaps it, we speak of _____ conditioning.

delayed

- -

31

DEFINE delayed conditioning:

a. The CS precedes the US by _____.

a long interval (an interval longer than 5 seconds)

b. The CS and the US _____.

overlap
(or equivalent answers)

- -

32

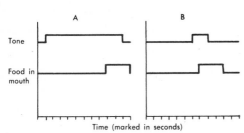

Tone

Food in mouth

Time (marked in seconds)

Which illustration represents simultaneous conditioning? ____

The other diagram illustrates _____ _____.

- -

33

Pavlov and other workers found that conditioning could be carried out by the delayed pairing procedure. They found it harder to do, and less effective, than _____ conditioning.

- -

34

Delayed conditioning becomes more difficult as the interval between the *CS* and the *US* becomes _____.

- -

35

At the very beginning of a delayed conditioning experiment, the *CS* (initially a neutral stimulus) is presented, say for 15 seconds. At the end of 15 seconds, we present the ____.

The *US* elicits the _____.

- -

B
delayed conditioning

simultaneous

greater *or* longer

US
response

36

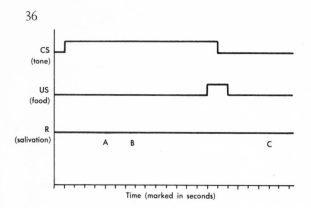

At the beginning of the experiment, the response would be elicited by the *US* and appear in position _____ (letter).

After a number of pairings, the *CS* will elicit the response with a *short* latency, and the response would appear in position _____.

However, after a very large number of pairings with the same delay interval, the response occurs with a longer latency to the *CS* but still prior to the *US*. Therefore, *R* will occur in position _____.

C

A

B

37

As a consequence of the delayed conditioning procedure, the response appears in the time interval between the onset of the _____ and the onset of the _____.

CS
US

38

Early in conditioning, as the CS acquires the power to elicit the response, the response begins to appear:

☐ soon after the CS is presented

☐ just before the US is presented

But after prolonged exposure to the delayed conditioning procedure, the response appears:

☐ soon after the CS is presented

☐ with a longer latency to the CS, but prior to the US

soon after the CS is presented

with a longer latency to the CS, but prior to the US

39

On the first conditioning trial (i.e., the first pairing) when the CS is presented, the response:

☐ occurs

☐ does not occur

does not occur

40

In early trials using the delayed conditioning procedure, the response occurs (☐ early ☐ late) in the CS interval.

early

41

With prolonged training using delayed conditioning, the response occurs (☐ closer to ☐ farther from) the US.

closer to

42

So, as delayed conditioning proceeds, the latency of the response to the CS is initially (☐ long ☐ short) and later becomes (☐ longer ☐ shorter).

short longer

43

With prolonged delayed conditioning, the latency of the response to the CS still remains shorter than the interval between the CS and the _____.

US

- -

44

We have discussed two conditioning procedures. They are called _____ conditioning and _____ conditioning.

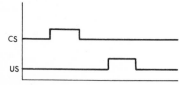

Does this diagram fit the definition of either of these two procedures?

☐ yes
☐ no

simultaneous
delayed
(either order)

no

- -

45

Here is an illustration of *trace conditioning*:

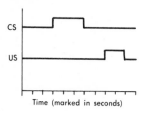

Time (marked in seconds)

Do the two stimuli ever overlap in trace conditioning?

☐ yes
☐ no

This procedure is different from simultaneous or delayed conditioning because the CS termination:

☐ precedes the *US* onset
☐ follows the *US* onset

no

precedes the *US* onset

- -

46

In trace conditioning, the CS and the US:

    □ must overlap

    □ must not overlap

must not overlap

- -

47

Which of the following statements is an example of the procedure for trace conditioning?

    □ The smell of food precedes its taste.

    □ The click of cocking a pistol precedes the sound of its firing.

The click of cocking a pistol precedes the sound of its firing.

- -

48

When the CS precedes but does *not* overlap the US, we speak of _____ conditioning.

trace

- -

49

DESCRIBE the trace conditioning procedure.

_____

In trace conditioning, the CS precedes the US and does not overlap the US.

- -

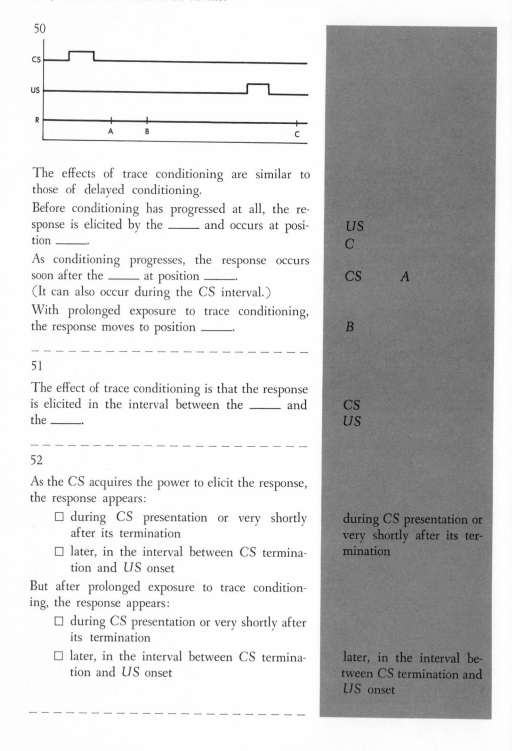

The effects of trace conditioning are similar to those of delayed conditioning.

Before conditioning has progressed at all, the response is elicited by the _____ and occurs at position _____.

  US
  C

As conditioning progresses, the response occurs soon after the _____ at position _____.
(It can also occur during the CS interval.)

  CS A

With prolonged exposure to trace conditioning, the response moves to position _____.

  B

––––––––––––––––––––––––––––––

51

The effect of trace conditioning is that the response is elicited in the interval between the _____ and the _____.

  CS
  US

––––––––––––––––––––––––––––––

52

As the CS acquires the power to elicit the response, the response appears:

 ☐ during CS presentation or very shortly after its termination

 ☐ later, in the interval between CS termination and US onset

during CS presentation or very shortly after its termination

But after prolonged exposure to trace conditioning, the response appears:

 ☐ during CS presentation or very shortly after its termination

 ☐ later, in the interval between CS termination and US onset

later, in the interval between CS termination and US onset

––––––––––––––––––––––––––––––

53

So, as trace conditioning proceeds, the latency of the response to the CS first is (□ long   □ short), and later becomes (□ longer   □ shorter).

short
longer

54

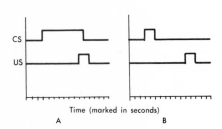

Time (marked in seconds)

A   B

Procedure *A* shows _____ conditioning.

Procedure *B* shows _____ conditioning.

delay *or* delayed

trace

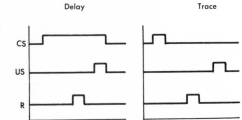

Delay   Trace

55

In which procedure does the response come to occur at a time when no stimulus is present?

_____

in trace conditioning

56

With which procedure would it be *most* difficult to produce Pavlovian conditioning? _____

trace conditioning

– –

57

Pavlov found trace conditioning to be the most difficult to obtain.

The next most difficult procedure was _____ conditioning.

delayed

The easiest procedure was _____ conditioning.

simultaneous

– –

58

What is the most effective temporal arrangement of stimuli for producing conditioning?

    ☐ strictly simultaneous presentation of CS and *US*

    ☐ CS precedes the *US* by ¼ second to 2 seconds and overlaps the *US*

    ☐ CS precedes but does not overlap the *US*

CS precedes the US by ¼ second to 2 seconds and overlaps the *US*

– –

59

Each of the diagrams below represents a stage in the training of an animal using trace conditioning procedures. The order of the diagrams is rearranged.

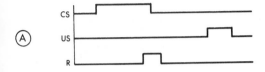

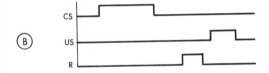

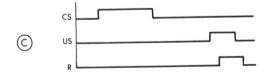

Which diagram represents:

an early stage in trace conditioning? _____

a later stage in trace conditioning? _____

the latest stage in trace conditioning? _____

C

A

B

60

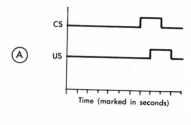

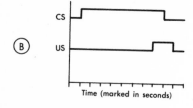

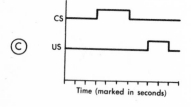

Illustration A represents the procedure for ———————— conditioning.

Illustration B represents the procedure for ———————— conditioning.

Illustration C represents the procedure for ———————— conditioning.

simultaneous

delayed

trace

R-9

Higher Order Conditioning

READ THROUGH PANEL R-9-1 BEFORE GOING ON TO THE FIRST ITEM.

- -

1

(Refer to Panel R-9-1, paragraph 1.)

The *US* in initial conditioning is _____.

food in the mouth

- -

2

(Refer to Panel R-9-1, paragraph 1.)

The original *CS* is a _____.

light

- -

3

(Refer to Panel R-9-1, paragraph 1.)

Before conditioning, the neutral stimulus (light) is called *by Pavlov* an "_____ _____."

"indifferent agent"

- -

4

(Refer to Panel R-9-1, paragraph 1.)

DRAW the paradigm for the conditioning described in paragraph 1. (Do not use symbols; write out the actual stimuli and response.)

food in mouth ⟶ salivation

light ⟋

- -

5

(Refer to Panel R-9-1, paragraph 1.)

The light was on for how long? _____

one-half minute

Although it is not specifically stated, the light was on when the food presentation began. Which of these diagrams illustrates the procedure Pavlov used?

CS

US

A

Time
(in ten-second units)

CS

US

B

Time
(in ten-second units)

CS

US

C

Time
(in ten-second units)

A

6

REVIEW FRAME

CHECK the appropriate boxes below:

	Simultaneous	Delay	Trace
CS onset precedes US onset	☐	☐	☐
CS and US overlap	☐	☐	☐
CS termination precedes US onset	☐	☐	☐
CS termination follows US onset	☐	☐	☐
CS onset follows US onset	☐	☐	☐

	Simultaneous	Delay	Trace
	☒	☒	☒
	☒	☒	☐
	☐	☐	☒
	☒	☒	☐
	☐	☐	☐

- -

7

(Refer to Panel R-9-1, paragraph 1.)

Thus, the conditioned reflex was an example of a (☐ simultaneous ☐ delayed ☐ trace) conditioning procedure.

delayed

- -

8

(Refer to Panel R-9-1, paragraph 2.)

Following initial conditioning, the magnitude of the salivary response to the light was _____ drops.

10

- -

9

(Refer to Panel R-9-1, paragraph 2.)

A new stimulus, a _____, was then added and was paired with the _____.

tone
light *or* CS

- -

10

(Refer to Panel R-9-1, paragraph 2.)

Was the combination tone-light paired with food?
□ yes   □ no

no

- -

11

(Refer to Panel R-9-1, paragraph 2.)

Therefore, we can assume that before conditioning the tone was initially a (□ neutral   □ conditioned) stimulus.

neutral

- -

12

(Refer to Panel R-9-1, paragraph 2.)

When the tone and light were first paired, they
produced a response of a magnitude (□ less than
□ the same as   □ greater than) the response
produced by the light alone.

the same as

- -

13

(Refer to Panel R-9-1, paragraph 2.)

After several pairings with the light, what power
did the tone acquire? _____

the power to elicit salivation
(or equivalent answer)

- -

14

(Refer to Panel R-9-1, paragraph 2.)

The effect of pairing the tone and light was that
the tone elicited a response whose magnitude was
_____ drops.

1 or 2

- -

15

(Refer to Panel R-9-1, paragraph 2.)

The magnitude of the response to the tone was (□ less □ more) than the response to the light alone.

less

- -

16

(Refer to Panel R-9-1, paragraph 2.)

It was demonstrated that the tone did become a(n) _____ stimulus, although the magnitude of the response to the tone was (□ less than □ greater than) it was to the light.

conditioned
less than

- -

17

(Refer to Panel R-9-1, paragraph 3.)

Pavlov reports not only that the magnitude of the response to the tone is less, but also that "if the experiments are continued for some time _____." (COMPLETE the sentence.)

the tone will lose its action

- -

18

(Refer to Panel R-9-1.)

The conditioning procedure that Pavlov describes in paragraphs 2 and 3 is called _____ order conditioning.

second

- -

19

(Refer to Panel R-9-1.)

There seems to be, then, an additional phenomenon of conditioned reflexes: a neutral stimulus (a tone) has become a conditioned stimulus in spite of the fact that it has never been paired directly with the _____.

US or unconditioned stimulus *or* food in the mouth

- -

20

(Refer to Panel R-9-1.)

The tone acquired the power to elicit a response by being paired with another _____ stimulus (a light).

conditioned

— — — — — — — — — — — — — — — — — —

21

(Refer to Panel R-9-1.)

The tone is referred to as a conditioned stimulus of the _____ order.

second

— — — — — — — — — — — — — — — — — —

22

A paradigm describing this procedure of second order conditioning would be:

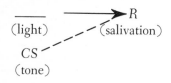

$$\underline{\quad\quad} \longrightarrow R$$
(light)   (salivation)
CS
(tone)

CS ⟶ R
(light)   (salivation)
CS
(tone)

— — — — — — — — — — — — — — — — — —

23

(Refer to Panel R-9-1, paragraph 3.)

The reflex: tone ⟶ salivation is called a reflex of the _____ _____.

second order

— — — — — — — — — — — — — — — — — —

24

A conditioned reflex can be established in two ways:

1. by pairing a conditioned stimulus with an unconditioned stimulus
2. _____

by pairing a conditioned stimulus with a previously conditioned stimulus (or equivalent answer)

— — — — — — — — — — — — — — — — — —

25

If an initially neutral stimulus is paired with a conditioned stimulus, the neutral stimulus can become a stimulus of the _____ order, and the resultant reflex is called a _____.

second
reflex of the second order

- -

26

One important characteristic of a second order reflex is that the magnitude of the response is considerably (☐ less ☐ greater) than the magnitude of the response in a first order reflex.

less

- -

27

Magnitude and latency are inversely related. That means that as magnitude decreases, latency _____.

increases

- -

28

If the magnitude of the response to the second order CS is smaller than the magnitude of the response to the first order CS, you might predict that the latency of the response to the second order CS would be (☐ shorter ☐ longer) than that to the first order CS.

longer

- -

29

Another property of a second order reflex is that if the experiment is continued for some time, the response to the second order CS will _____.

disappear *or* drop out *or* lose its action *or* decrease (or equivalent answer)

- -

30

(Refer to Panel R-9-1.)

What happened to the magnitude of the response as the experiment progressed from lower order to higher order conditioning?

The magnitude:

☐ increased

☐ decreased

decreased

31

The transitory nature of the second order reflex and the small magnitude of the response led Pavlov to raise some doubt as to the actual existence of second order reflexes.

NO RESPONSE REQUIRED

NO RESPONSE REQUIRED; GO ON TO NEXT FRAME.

32

One or two of Pavlov's pupils have reported third and higher order conditioned reflexes. A third order conditioned reflex would require that an initially neutral stimulus be paired only with a conditioned stimulus of the _____ order.

second

33

Experiments in recent years have not been able to reproduce these experiments on conditioned reflexes above the second order. Considering Pavlov's statements and these recent findings, the existence of higher order reflexes is (☐ likely ☐ unlikely).

unlikely

34

Now you should be able to design a complex conditioning experiment.

You are given a dog, a supply of food powder, a buzzer to become the first order CS, and a black cardboard square. You are going to make the square into a second order CS. Your very *first* step toward eventually obtaining a second order conditioned reflex would be to form a conditioned reflex between the _____ and _____.

buzzer (and) food in the mouth

- -

35

After the buzzer had acquired the eliciting power of a CS, the next step would be to _____.

pair the black square with the buzzer

- -

36

To demonstrate clearly and unquestionably that you had produced *second order* conditioning, you must be careful never to pair the _____ _____ with the _____.

black square
food in the mouth (*US*)

- -

37

By the way, there is something else you should have done. You should have shown that *before* conditioning, neither the buzzer nor the black square _____ salivation.

elicited

- -

38

To show that the buzzer and square were originally neutral stimuli, you could, in test trials before conditioning, present the buzzer or black square and observe if _____ occurred.

salivation

- -

39

If no salivation occurred, then you could properly state: "The CS's were originally _____ stimuli."

neutral

40

To review: All the conditioning procedures that we have described thus far have one important feature in common: in every case, there is pairing between two _____.

stimuli

41

To obtain the simple first order conditioned reflex, it is necessary to pair _____.

a CS with a US

42

Two steps are involved in the formation of a second order conditioned reflex. First, a CS is paired with a US until a conditioned reflex is formed. Second, _____.

a new CS is paired with the CS until this CS acquires eliciting power (or equivalent answer)

43

By definition, a neutral stimulus will not elicit the response prior to _____.

conditioning

44

The whole object of the conditioning procedure is to form a _____ reflex. We know that conditioning has taken place when a stimulus which was initially _____ has acquired the eliciting power of, and can be substituted for, the _____.

new *or* conditioned

neutral

US

45

We know we have a conditioned reflex when the CS _____ the _____.

elicits (the) response *or* R

46

The response is measured in terms of its _____ and its _____.

latency } either
magnitude } order

47

REVIEW

CHECK the appropriate box to indicate whether each of the following variables is dependent or independent:

	Dependent	Independent
Latency	☐	☐
Magnitude	☐	☐
Number of pairings	☐	☐
Order of conditioning	☐	☐
Intensity	☐	☐

	Dependent	Independent
Latency	☒	☐
Magnitude	☒	☐
Number of pairings	☐	☒
Order of conditioning	☐	☒
Intensity	☐	☒

48

Thus far we have dealt with many stimuli and many responses.

There are more stimuli and responses in this and the following frames. You will be asked to INDICATE whether there is a reflex, and, if there is, to COMPLETE the paradigm for it by giving the specific stimulus and response, and indicating if the stimulus is a US or a CS.

For example:

> A small child gets smoke in his eyes while standing near a bonfire and his eyes water.

Is this a reflex? □ yes □ no

If it is a reflex, COMPLETE the paradigm for it below:

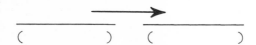

(   )   (   )

- - - - - - - - - - - - - - - - - - - -

49

> A boy runs away from a dog.

Is this a reflex? □ yes □ no

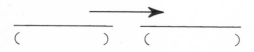

(   )   (   )

> The sound of the dentist's drill causes a man to perspire.

Is this a reflex? □ yes □ no

(   )   (   )

- - - - - - - - - - - - - - - - - - - -

yes

$US \longrightarrow R$
(smoke) (eyes water)
(or equivalent answer)

no

yes

$CS \longrightarrow R$
(sound of (perspiring)
drill)
(or equivalent answer)

50

Here is a brief description of an incident:

> As it was growing dark and cold, two boys were playing a game of catch. The cold wind raised "goose bumps" on their arms. Soon, their mother called them for dinner. When they heard her, they began to run to the house and their mouths began to water. As they entered the brightly lit house, their pupils, which had expanded in the dark, contracted in the light. As they were seated at dinner, one of them spilled a glass of milk. When their dessert was brought, the boys grabbed for it, and as a result their mother scolded them.

Now, DIAGRAM the reflexes in the incident described.

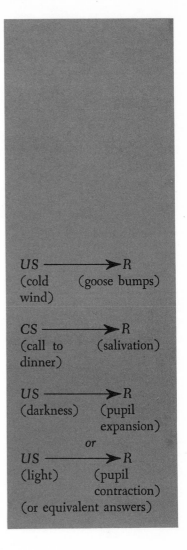

US ⟶ R
(cold   (goose bumps)
wind)

CS ⟶ R
(call to   (salivation)
dinner)

US ⟶ R
(darkness)   (pupil
             expansion)

or

US ⟶ R
(light)   (pupil
             contraction)

(or equivalent answers)

Epilogue on Reflex Conditioning

by Fred S. Keller

YOU have just been introduced, in a very up-to-date way, to one of the most basic ideas and one of the most important principles known to modern psychology—the concept of the reflex and the law of Pavlovian conditioning. If the introduction was painless and everything seemed quite simple, good! Learning does not have to hurt to be real, and some of the most powerful ideas are also the simplest.

However, these materials did not always seem so simple. From Descartes, the 11th century mathematician and natural philosopher, to Sherrington, the 20th century physiologist, it took about 300 years to make the concept of the reflex as clear as it is today; and Pavlov spent half his lifetime of research in pinning down the facts that help us understand why a hungry dog will secrete saliva at the sight of his food dish—showing us how new reflexes are established through conditioning.

Today, there remain many questions to be asked about conditioning. Some of them are very specific and of interest mainly to the laboratory worker, but others are quite general. For example: Does the conditioned reflex account for *all* learning? Pavlov thought that the answer was, "Yes," and many people have agreed with him, including some well-known American psychologists. John B. Watson, the colorful and aggressive founder of "Behaviorism" in American psychology, early adopted Pavlov's law and regarded it as the key to all habit-formation. Edwin R. Guthrie, another Behaviorist, was also influenced by Pavlov, but used the notion Stimulus-Response pairing rather than Stimulus-Stimulus pairing, as basic to all modification of behavior. You could do worse than read either Watson or Guthrie, for effective style as well as content. But don't stop there; do the rest of this program before you decide that Pavlovian conditioning is the answer to every question.

Certainly, by applying the principles of Pavlovian conditioning, we can begin to see why a man perspires at the buzz of a dentist's drill, why his pulse quickens on receiving good news, or why his breathing is upset by the sound of a midnight prowler—indeed, why he responds emotionally to a thousand other stimulus situations. However, we may not be ready to say with Guthrie that *all* learning is of the same kind, especially when we are dealing with that great body of behavior which seems to be acquired because of the *results achieved,* rather than the stimuli that elicit them. Pavlov's principle explains why a dog in its lab harness will salivate at the sound of a bell, but it may not explain quite so easily why the animal runs and jumps into his harness before the bell is sounded. This is the sort of learning we'll take up next.

With your present background, you are now ready to go more deeply into the story of reflex conditioning on your own. You would enjoy especially the first two chapters (maybe more) of Pavlov's own *Conditioned Reflexes,*[1] one of the great books of our century. You would also appreciate, as mentioned before, Watson's use of Pavlov's principle [2] and Guthrie's attempt [3] to modify and extend it in various directions—not entirely with Pavlov's approval. If your interest is strongly biological, you might like to sample part of Sherrington's classic work on the reflex,[4] but perhaps right now you'd better wait until you've finished with this text: there is more conditioning to come!

Fred S. Keller
Professor of Psychology
University of Arizona

[1] Pavlov, I. P., *Conditioned Reflexes.* New York: Dover Press, 1960.

[2] Watson, J. B., *Behaviorism.* New York: Phoenix Press.

[3] Guthrie, E. R., *The Psychology of Learning.* New York: Harper, 1935, 1952 revised.

[4] Sherrington, Sir Charles, *The Integrative Action of the Nervous System.* New Haven: Yale University Press, 1961.

Part 2

OPERANT CONDITIONING

O-1

Operant Behavior

1

REVIEW FRAME

We have analyzed the environment into parts, or changes, called _____.

We have also analyzed behavior into parts, or changes, called _____.

stimuli

responses

— — — — — — — — — — — — — — — — — — — —

2

REVIEW FRAME

We have seen that a certain part of our behavior is elicited by stimuli.

This kind of predictable relationship between stimuli and responses is called a(n) _____.

reflex

— — — — — — — — — — — — — — — — — — — —

3

REVIEW FRAME

In a reflex, the first event is the _____.

The second event is the _____.

stimulus

response

— — — — — — — — — — — — — — — — — — — —

4

REVIEW FRAME

In a reflex, which stimuli precede the response?

□ *US's* only

□ *CS's* only

□ both

□ neither

both

— — — — — — — — — — — — — — — — — — — —

5

REVIEW FRAME

In reflex conditioning, we pair what two kinds of stimuli? _____

- -

CS (or neutral stimulus) and US (either order)

6

After conditioning, an additional stimulus comes to control the response that originally was controlled only by the *US*. This new stimulus is called the _____.

- -

CS

7

After conditioning, we may substitute the _____ stimulus for the _____ stimulus and elicit a similar response.

- -

conditioned
unconditioned

8

DRAW the paradigm for the newly established reflex.

- -

CS ⟶ R

9

CASE I	CASE II
Food powder is placed in a dog's mouth. He salivates.	A child calls. His mother runs to him, picks him up, and cuddles him.

In the above case, a change in the external environment elicited a response from the organism.

In the above case, a response by an organism (child) produced a change in the external environment (mother comes, etc.).

In the examples below, INDICATE whether the example most resembles Case I or Case II. (CHECK your answer after each example.)

	I	II	I	II
a. A dog received a piece of candy each time he sat up.	☐	☐	☐	☒
b. Your pupils enlarged as you stood in the rear of a darkened movie theater.	☐	☐	☒	☐
c. As a result of continued running, her heart beat faster.	☐	☐	☒	☐
d. He struck out savagely, toppling his opponent to the floor.	☐	☐	☐	☒
e. Stark fear made his pupils dilate and sweat stand out on his brow.	☐	☐	☒	☐
f. "Give me another helping of mashed potatoes, please," he said, and was served.	☐	☐	☐	☒
g. The mere mention of steak made his mouth water.	☐	☐	☒	☐
h. He put on his glasses and saw the sign clearly.	☐	☐	☐	☒
i. The wolf huffed and puffed and blew the house down.	☐	☐	☐	☒

The previous sections of this program have dealt with stimulus-response relationships such as the one described in (☐ Case I ☐ Case II).

Case I

10

As the psychologist B. F. Skinner has written:

> "Reflexes, conditioned or otherwise, are mainly concerned with the internal physiology of the organism. We are most often interested, however, in behavior which has some effect upon the surrounding world."
>
> Skinner, B. F., *Science and Human Behavior,* p. 59.

It is to this second type of behavior that we now turn our attention.

NO RESPONSE REQUIRED

NO RESPONSE REQUIRED; GO ON TO NEXT FRAME

_ _

11

A man may crook his finger in a certain way. He may be firing a pistol, or he may be beckoning someone toward him.

Crooking the finger is an example of:

☐ behavior
☐ the effects of behavior

behavior

The pistol shot or the approach of the person beckoned to are examples of:

☐ behavior
☐ the effects of behavior

the effects of behavior

_ _

12

"Crooking the finger fired the gun."
"Crooking the finger summoned her to him."
"Stepping on the brake pedal slowed the car down."
"Stepping on the gas pedal speeded up the car."

In all four cases above, which came first in time?

☐ behavior
☐ effects

behavior

Which came second in time?

☐ behavior
☐ effects

effects

_ _

13

"Crooking the finger . . ."

"Stepping on the pedal . . ."

We will characterize the two bits of behavior described above by the familiar term responses.

From the description of a response alone, can you tell what its effects will be? ☐ yes ☐ no

no

— — — — — — — — — — — — — — — — — — — —

14

". . . firing of the gun."

". . . slowing of the car."

The effects of behavior listed above take place in the environment. These changes in the environment occur (☐ before ☐ after) the responses that produced them.

after

Changes in the environment are called _____.

stimuli

— — — — — — — — — — — — — — — — — — — —

15

Steve hit the window with his fist
and the window broke into pieces.

Which sentence below describes the sequence of events?

☐ A stimulus was followed by a response.

☐ A response was followed by a stimulus.

A response was followed by a stimulus

— — — — — — — — — — — — — — — — — — — —

16

FOOTNOTE FRAME

Many times, a response that results in a change in the environment is preceded by a stimulus that can be specified. Other times, this is not the case.

For example, if a man steps on the gas pedal after a traffic light turns green, we can specify the stimulus with a fair degree of certainty. In the case of a baby waving its arms in the air, we might have more difficulty determining the stimulus.

For purposes of analyzing behavior at this time, we will not deal with the question of preceding stimuli, but only with the effects of responses.

NO RESPONSE REQUIRED

NO RESPONSE REQUIRED; GO ON TO NEXT FRAME

_ _ _ _ _ _ _ _ _ _ _ _ _ _ _ _ _ _ _ _

17

When we describe behavior that alters the environment, we write:

$R \longrightarrow S$

The arrow ($\longrightarrow$) is read *is followed by*.
WRITE the sentence summarized by the paradigm
$R \longrightarrow S$. _____

A response is followed by a stimulus.

_ _ _ _ _ _ _ _ _ _ _ _ _ _ _ _ _ _ _ _

18

For each of the following sentences, CHECK the appropriate paradigm:

"The sight of the menu elicits salivation."

☐ $R \longrightarrow S$
☐ $S \longrightarrow R$

"Pressing the doorbell is followed by ringing."

☐ $R \longrightarrow S$
☐ $S \longrightarrow R$

"Turning the faucet is followed by water running."

☐ $R \longrightarrow S$
☐ $S \longrightarrow R$

_ _ _ _ _ _ _ _ _ _ _ _ _ _ _ _ _ _ _ _

19

In the paradigm $S \longrightarrow R$, the arrow means _____, while in the paradigm $R \longrightarrow S$, the arrow means _____.

	elicits
	is followed by

20

Stepping, crooking (the finger), and hitting are all rough descriptions of a kind of behavior that has effects on the environment. Because such behavior "operates" on the environment, it is technically called *operant* behavior.

Which response(s) is/are probably operant behavior?

    ☐ contracting of pupils

    ☐ hitting a window pane   hitting a window pane

    ☐ salivating

    ☐ turning a key   turning a key

21

Which of the following phrases describe(s) a response operating on the environment?

    ☐ hitting a typewriter key   hitting a typewriter key

    ☐ increase in blood pressure

    ☐ pulling a voting booth lever   pulling a voting booth lever

    ☐ turning a steering wheel   turning a steering wheel

22

$R \longrightarrow S$ is the paradigm for:

    ☐ operant behavior   operant behavior

    ☐ reflex behavior

$S \longrightarrow R$ is the paradigm for:

    ☐ operant behavior

    ☐ reflex behavior   reflex behavior

23

$$R \longrightarrow S$$

WRITE the sentence that is summarized by the above paradigm. _____

A response is followed by a stimulus.
(or equivalent answer)

For what kind of behavior is this a paradigm? _____

operant (behavior)

This kind of behavior derives its name from the fact that it _____ on the environment.

operates

_ _

24

DRAW and IDENTIFY the paradigms for both reflex and operant behavior:

$$R \longrightarrow S: \text{operant}$$
$$S \longrightarrow R: \text{reflex}$$

_ _

25

We gave the eliciting paradigm

$$S \longrightarrow R$$

the name *reflex*.

A useful name for our new paradigm

$$R \longrightarrow S$$

is *contingency*. To be contingent means "to be dependent upon." In a contingency, the occurrence of a(n) _____ is dependent or contingent upon the occurrence of a(n) _____.

stimulus (S)
response (R)

_ _

26

$$R \longrightarrow S$$

The paradigm above shows that the occurrence of the stimulus is dependent upon the occurrence of the response.

Thus, we call this paradigm a(n) _____.

contingency

_ _

27

The sentences below are various ways of describing an operant contingency. WRITE the abbreviations "*R*" and "*S*" in the proper blanks in each sentence:

The _____ is followed by the _____.

The _____ is produced by the _____.

If _____, then _____.

The _____ is the result of the _____.

R	*S*
S	*R*
R	*S*
S	*R*

28

Operant behavior is behavior that can alter, or produce effects upon, the _____.

environment

29

We can describe any particular operant response and its consequences by adding descriptions under the letters in our paradigm. For example:

R———————▶ S
(moving   (Light
light   illuminates
switch   room.)
to "on")

DRAW and LABEL a paradigm for the statement "Dialing ME 7-1212 is followed by the recorded announcement of the time": _____

R———————▶ S
(dial-   (time
ing ME   announce-
7-1212)   ment)

30

In this paradigm

$$R \longrightarrow S$$
(press   (doorbell
button)   rings)

pressing the button is an example of:
- ☐ behavior
- ☐ an effect of environment

The ringing of the doorbell is an example of:
- ☐ behavior
- ☐ an effect on the environment

behavior

an effect on the environment

- -

31

In the paradigm for operant behavior:

$R \longrightarrow S$, we say: "The response
_____ an effect on the environment."

produces *or* is followed by
(or equivalent answer)

- -

32

DEFINE operant behavior. _____

Operant behavior is behavior that produces an effect on, or operates on, the environment.
(or equivalent answer)

DRAW the paradigm for operant behavior:
_____

$$R \longrightarrow S$$

- -

33

Some consequences of operant behavior increase the frequency of that behavior.

For example, if in the past a student has received good grades for studying, is it likely that he will study more frequently in the future? ☐ yes ☐ no

yes

If a child's mother has in the past consistently torn up a child's drawings, is it likely that he will give them to her more frequently in the future? ☐ yes ☐ no

no

If a child is praised each time he practices good table manners, is it likely that he will practice them more frequently in the future? ☐ yes ☐ no

yes

_ _

34

Suppose that a baby is shaking an *empty* rattle in its hand. Then we have the following $R \longrightarrow S$ contingency:

    R: shaking
    S: rattle moves

WRITE the abbreviations "R" and "S" in the proper paradigm with subscript descriptions.

───────────────

$R \longrightarrow S$
(shaking   (rattle
rattle)   moves)

If we now insert small pebbles or shot into the rattle so that it makes noise when the baby shakes it, we will have changed (☐ the effect of the response ☐ the response).

the effect of the response

After this change, the baby would probably shake the rattle (☐ more often ☐ less often).

more often

_ _

35

In the example of the baby and the rattle, we changed the _____ that the R produced.

The result of this change was that the frequency of the R:

    ☐ increased

    ☐ decreased

S *or* effects *or* consequence

increased

- -

36

When the consequences of operant behavior increase the frequency of that behavior, we call such consequences *reinforcing stimuli*.

Reinforcing stimuli:

    ☐ follow operant behavior

    ☐ precede operant behavior

follow operant behavior

- -

37

When we reinforce an army with troops or concrete with steel, we make them both:

    ☐ stronger

    ☐ weaker

stronger

- -

38

Similarly, when psychologists speak of reinforcing a response, they refer to a procedure which makes that response _____.

stronger

- -

39

Thus, a reinforcing stimulus would be one that:

    ☐ strengthens a response

    ☐ weakens a response

strengthens a response

- -

40

We know that a stimulus is reinforcing if the response which produces it begins to occur:

☐ less often
☐ more often

more often

41

In our example, the frequency of the baby's response of "shaking the rattle" increased when pebbles were added.

In this example, the reinforcing stimulus was
_____.

noise *or* rattling sound

42

We can add to our paradigm:
$$R \longrightarrow S^R$$
(shaking   (noise)
rattle)

The *superscript* R in the symbol S^R, stands for "reinforcing." (It does not stand for "response.") In our example, then, noise is a(n) _____ stimulus because it (☐ increases ☐ decreases) the frequency of the response.

reinforcing
increases

43

If an S is a reinforcing stimulus, we add the superscript _____.

R

44

What do these symbols stand for?

R _____
S^R _____

response
reinforcing stimulus

45

A reinforcing stimulus is designated by the symbol _____.

S^R

- -

46

For any bit of operant behavior:

$$R \longrightarrow S$$

we can add the superscript R:

$$R \longrightarrow S^R$$

if the effect of the stimulus is to:

☐ increase the frequency of R

increase the frequency of R

☐ decrease the frequency of R

- -

47

The effect of a reinforcing stimulus is to increase the _____ of a response that produces that stimulus.

frequency

WRITE the paradigm for this relationship between S^R and R. _____

$$R \longrightarrow S^R$$

- -

48

Any operant contingency can be printed as:

$$R \longrightarrow S$$

We only write:

$$R \longrightarrow S^R$$

if the stimulus is a(n) _____.

reinforcer

We determine when we can add the superscript R by observing whether or not the response, when followed by S, _____.

increases in frequency (or equivalent answer)

- -

49

If applause is a reinforcer for telling jokes, WRITE a paradigm that describes the contingency in detail. _____

$$R \longrightarrow S^R$$
(telling   (applause)
jokes)

- -

50

WRITE the general paradigm that shows the relationship between S and R that increases the frequency of R. _____

Now WRITE the paradigm in sentence form.
_____

$$R \longrightarrow S^R$$

The response is followed by the reinforcement. (or equivalent answer)

- -

51

What is the effect of a reinforcing contingency upon an operant response? _____

The operant response increases in frequency. (or equivalent answer)

- -

52

Suppose that you wanted to train your dog to roll over. You could do this by giving him a pellet of food:

    ☐ each time he rolled over

    ☐ once every minute

each time he rolled over

- -

53

His rolling over would increase because getting food pellets:

☐ would be contingent upon his rolling over response

☐ would not be contingent upon his rolling over response

would be contingent upon his rolling over response

- -

54

Giving the dog a food pellet each time he rolls over:

☐ is a contingency

☐ is not a contingency

is a contingency

Giving the dog a food pellet once every minute:

☐ is a contingency

☐ is not a contingency

is not a contingency

Which procedure will strengthen the behavior of rolling over?

☐ giving the dog a food pellet each time he rolls over

giving the dog a food pellet each time he rolls over

☐ giving the dog a food pellet once every minute

- -

55

To be called a reinforcer, what effect must the food pellet have on the response? _____

It must increase the frequency of that response.

- -

56

The procedure for operant conditioning is to set up a situation in which a reinforcing stimulus is _____ upon the occurrence of a response.

contingent

- -

57

WRITE the general paradigm for the procedure that increases the frequency of an operant response. _____

$$R \longrightarrow S^R$$

— — — — — — — — — — — — — — — — — — — —

58

CHECK each of the following as applying to operant behavior or to reflex behavior:

	Operant	Reflex		
CS	☐	☐	☐	☒
higher-order conditioning	☐	☐	☐	☒
pairing of stimuli	☐	☐	☐	☒
reinforcement follows the response	☐	☐	☒	☐
response operates on the environment	☐	☐	☒	☐
stimulus elicits response	☐	☐	☐	☒
stimulus is contingent upon response	☐	☐	☒	☐
stimulus precedes response	☐	☐	☐	☒
S^R	☐	☐	☒	☐
US	☐	☐	☐	☒

O-2

Operant Conditioning

1

The frequency of a small child saying "da-da" is increased when saying "da-da" is followed by attention from the child's parents.

What is the reinforcement? _____

What is the response? _____

attention

saying "da-da"

- -

2

(Look at Panel O-2-1.)

What animal is inside the apparatus? _____

What is the operant response? _____

What is the reinforcer? _____

a pigeon

key-peck

grain

- -

3

(Refer to Panel O-2-1.)

The response, a peck on the key, is followed by _____.

DRAW the complete paradigm that shows the contingency employed in this experiment.

_____

grain *or* reinforcement

$$R \xrightarrow{\hspace{2cm}} S^R$$
(key-peck)   (grain)

- -

4

Below is a list of activities performed by the pigeon over a period of time. These responses follow each other very closely.

1. turns head toward back of chamber
2. turns head toward window of chamber
3. turns around
4. moves to far corner
5. goes to food aperture
6. moves to key
7. pecks key
8. turns around
9. moves to corner of chamber
10. moves to food aperture

If we make the grain available between activities 1 and 2, what response will be reinforced?

_____

What response will be strengthened if we reinforce between 8 and 9? _____

turning head toward back of chamber *or* no. 1

turning around *or* no. 8

– –

5

(Refer to Panel O-2-1.)

According to the contingency described, which response would be followed by grain? _____

key-peck *or* no. 7

– –

6

(Refer to Panel O-2-1.)

    1. turns head toward back of chamber
    2. turns head toward window of chamber
    3. turns around
    4. moves to far corner
    5. goes to food aperture
    6. moves to key
    7. pecks key
    8. turns around
    9. moves to corner of chamber
    10. moves to food aperture

In the experiment described in the panel, which response will be strengthened? _____

key-peck *or* no. 7

7

Below is a list of activities performed by the pigeon over a period of time. These responses follow each other very closely.

    1. turns head toward back of chamber
    2. turns head toward window of chamber
    3. turns around
    4. moves to far corner
    5. goes to food aperture
    6. moves to key
    7. pecks key
    8. turns around
    9. moves to corner of chamber
    10. moves to food aperture

If the reinforcement for key-pecking is delayed very slightly, the pigeon will move on to activity no. _____.

8

8

If the interval between the selected response and reinforcement is long, we will strengthen:

☐ no response
☐ the selected response
☐ another response

In order that the frequency of key-pecking increase, reinforcement must:

☐ follow the response of key-peck immediately
☐ follow the response of key-peck eventually
☐ occur before the key-peck response

another response

follow the response of key-peck immediately

- -

9

In operant conditioning, the reinforcement must follow the response (☐ eventually ☐ immediately).

Why? _____

immediately

If the reinforcement does not immediately follow the response, another response will be strengthened.
(or equivalent answer)

- -

10

(Look at Panel O-2-2.)

Shown in the panel is a record of a pigeon's key-pecking responses over a 20-minute period.

The paper moves 1 inch every _____ (how many) minutes.

The paper moves from:

☐ left to right
☐ right to left

5 (minutes)

right to left

- -

11

(Refer to Panel O-2-2.)

The paper in this response recorder moves 1 inch every 5 minutes. It moves at a:

☐ constant speed

☐ variable speed

Which came first in time?

☐ point *A*

☐ point *B*

☐ point *C*

☐ point *D*

constant speed

point A

12

(Refer to Panel O-2-2.)

The response being recorded is _____.

In what direction does the pen move when a response is made?

☐ down

☐ straight across

☐ up

In what direction does the pen move when no response is being made?

☐ down

☐ straight across

☐ up

key-pecking

up

straight across

13

Between points *A* and *B*, the pigeon made _____ (how many) response(s).

Between points *B* and *C*, the pigeon made:

☐ fewer responses than between points *A* and *B*

☐ more responses than between points *A* and *B*

☐ the same number of responses as between points *A* and *B*

☐ no responses

- -

14

Between points *C* and *D*, the pigeon made:

☐ few responses

☐ many responses

☐ no responses

- -

15

Rate means number per unit of time. For example, if a car travels 300 miles in 5 hours, the rate at which it traveled is 60 miles per hour.

$$\left(\frac{300 \text{ miles}}{5 \text{ hours}} = 60 \text{ miles per hour} \right)$$

(Now Refer to Panel O-2-2.)

FILL IN the numerator and denominator of the following fraction to indicate the rate of key-pecking during the first 5-minute period:

rate of responding = _____

- -

4

more responses than between points *A* and *B*

no responses

$$\frac{4 \text{ responses}}{5 \text{ minutes}} = 0.8 \text{ responses per minute}$$

16

(Refer to Panel O-2-2.)

At what rate did the pigeon respond during the second 5 minutes of time shown on the graph? _____ response(s) per minute.

$1.2 \left(\dfrac{6 \text{ responses}}{5 \text{ minutes}} \right)$

- -

17

(Refer to Panel O-2-2.)

NUMBER the four time intervals between the dotted lines (beginning with "1" to indicate the highest rate of responding, "2" to indicate the next highest rate, etc.)

_____ first time interval

_____ second time interval

_____ third time interval

_____ fourth time interval

2

1

3

4

- -

18

(Refer to Panel O-2-2.)

DETERMINE the rate of responses per minute for the 20-minute period shown. _____

0.65 (responses per minute)

- -

19

(Refer to Panel O-2-2.)

The word "cumulative" means "becoming larger by successive additions."

The device shown in the panel is called a "cumulative response recorder."

What is being successively added, i.e., cumulated?

_____

responses

- -

20

(Refer to Panel O-2-2.)

Assume that you wanted to show a cumulative response record to someone who had never seen one before. You would do well to label the axes of your record.

You would label the horizontal axis:

☐ Cumulative Responses

☐ Time

You would label the vertical axis _____.

Time

Cumulative Responses

21

LABEL the axes of the cumulative response record below:

Cumulative responses

Time

22

If we held a cumulative response record far enough away, we would not see the individual steps but only the general outline.

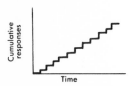

At a distance, the curve above would look like which one of the curves below? (CHECK ONE)

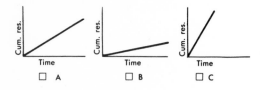

□ A   □ B   □ C

_A_

23

The general outline of a curve is called its *slope*.

DRAW the slope of (SMOOTH OUT) this curve:

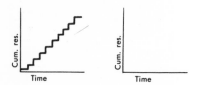

24

Which curve has the steeper slope? (CHECK ONE)

☐ A ☐ B

B

25

If an organism responds very rapidly, the slope of the curve becomes (☐ gradual ☐ steep).

steep

26

If only a few responses are made over a period of time, what will the slope of the curve look like? (CHECK ONE)

 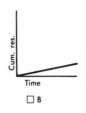

☐ A ☐ B ☐ C

B

27

Which curve shows the record of the more rapid rate of responding? (CHECK ONE)

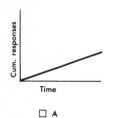 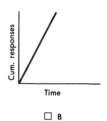

☐ A ☐ B

B

– – – – – – – – – – – – – – – – – – –

28

CHECK the appropriate box(es) in each case below:

	Rate of Responding		
	high	low	zero
zero slope (horizontal line)	☐	☐	☐
gradual slope	☐	☐	☐
steep slope	☐	☐	☐

Rate of Responding		
high	low	zero
☐	☐	☒
☐	☒	☐
☒	☐	☐

– – – – – – – – – – – – – – – – – – –

29

At what point does the rate begin to change?
☐ *A* ☐ *B* ☐ *C*

B

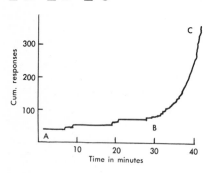

In which direction is the change?

  ☐ decrease in rate
  ☐ increase in rate

increase in rate

– – – – – – – – – – – – – – – – – – –

30

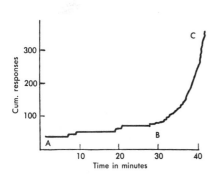

The frequency at which a response is emitted before a conditioning procedure is begun is called *operant level*. Referring to the cumulative response curve above, the first reinforcement was presented after about 27 minutes. What interval shows the operant level?

☐ *A-B*

☐ *B-C*

The response is emitted with greater frequency:

☐ before conditioning is begun

☐ after conditioning is begun

A-B

after conditioning is begun

31

At point *B* in the previous curve, reinforcement was begun. What effect did this new procedure have on the slope of the curve? _____

the slope became steeper (or equivalent answer)

32

In order to state that the rate increased as a result of the conditioning procedure, we must compare the rate during conditioning with the rate _____ conditioning.

before

33

Prior to performing an actual experiment to see if water is a reinforcing stimulus, we may place a thirsty rat in the box in order to determine the operant level. The operant level is the rate of responding *before* conditioning. In determining this level, we must:

☐ present water after each bar press

☐ present no water at all

present no water at all

- -

34

Suppose we are interested in studying the effects of milk presentation upon lever pressing in cats. We decide to measure response rate under two conditions:

a. when lever presses are ineffective in producing milk, and

b. when each lever press produces a drop of milk

The operant level would be determined under the conditions described in (☐ *a.* ☐ *b.*).

a.

- -

35

The operant level is the relative frequency at which an organism responds before conditioning takes place; it is thus measured in terms of _____ of responding.

rate

- -

36

Which of the following statements may be true if the experimenter does not determine the operant level rate before initiating the conditioning procedure?

☐ He cannot be sure that he is using a stimulus that reinforces.

☐ He cannot determine if the response rate has actually increased.

(Now Look at Panel O-2-3.)

What response was being reinforced? _____

What was the reinforcement? _____

The bar-press would not be reinforced during the:
☐ operant conditioning
☐ operant level

_____

37

If after determining an operant level rate, reinforcement is presented after each response, the response rate will:
☐ decrease
☐ increase

_____

38

Why is it important to determine an operant level rate? _____

_____

He cannot be sure that he is using a stimulus that reinforces.
He cannot determine if the response rate has actually increased.

bar-press

water *or* drop of water

operant level

increase

in order to be certain that an increase in response rate has occurred during conditioning
(or equivalent answer)

39

Another animal studied by psychologists is the monkey. In one type of experimental apparatus, the animal is harnessed in a chair and has a lever (telegraph key) to press. After each response, a bit of orange juice is delivered to the monkey.

If the rate of responding is increased, we can conclude that orange juice is a(n) _____.

reinforcer *or* reinforcing stimulus *or* S^R

_ _

40

(Look at Panel O-2-4.)

In this study the response being recorded is a(n) _____.

The subjects in the study were _____.

Each response was followed by _____.

lever press

children

candy

_ _

41

(Refer to Panel O-2-4.)

In the figure in this panel, the response rate is zero for the first 8 minutes. Then what happens to the rate? _____

It increases.
(or equivalent answer)

_ _

42

(Refer to Panel O-2-4.)

By the time 70 minutes had passed, the child had made about _____ (how many) responses.

600

_ _

43

(Refer to Panel O-2-4.)

This increase in rate indicates that, for this child, candy was a(n) _____.

reinforcer

_ _

44

(Refer to Panel O-2-4.)

In this study, as in the previous ones, a stimulus is presented immediately after each _____.

response

How do we know whether the stimulus we present is a reinforcer? _____

We know that it is a reinforcer if the rate of responding increases.
(or equivalent answer)

45

The pigeon pecking a key was presented with grain as a stimulus after each response. Since the response rate increased, we can call grain a(n) _____ for the pigeon.

reinforcer

46

(Refer to Panel O-2-4.)

In conditioning children, if the experimenters had used grain instead of candy, would the child's cumulative curve have looked like that shown in the figure?

☐ yes

☐ no

no

EXPLAIN your answer. _____

Grain would probably not act as a reinforcement for a child.
(or equivalent answer)

47

Will a stimulus that reinforces the behavior of an individual of one species necessarily reinforce the behavior of members of another species?

    ☐ yes

    ☐ no

no

- -

48

With both a thirsty child and a thirsty rat, water can probably be used as a(n) _____.

reinforcer *or* reinforcing stimulus *or* S^R

- -

49

Is it possible that a stimulus that reinforces the behavior of an individual of one species will also reinforce the behavior of another species?

    ☐ yes

    ☐ no

yes

- -

50

A rat may be reinforced by water, food, sexual activity, access to young, etc. One species, then, can be reinforced by:

    ☐ many stimuli

    ☐ very few stimuli

    ☐ no stimuli

many stimuli

Could more than one species be reinforced by food or water?

    ☐ yes

    ☐ no

yes

- -

51

We have dealt with several species of animals. Were we able to give evidence for operant conditioning in all cases?

☐ yes
☐ no

yes

- -

52

Suppose that we have built an apparatus in which to condition a whale. We have determined the whale's operant level for a given response, and we are ready to condition. What do we need?

_____

an effective reinforcement for a whale

How will we know when we have found what we need? _____

The rate of responding will increase.
(or equivalent answer)

- -

53

Let us again turn to the rat. The rate of bar-pressing increased when water was contingent upon the response.

What was the reinforcer? _____

water

WRITE the paradigm for increasing the rate of responding in this experiment (include the specific stimulus and response): _____

$$R \longrightarrow S^R$$
(bar-press)   (water)

- -

54

Could we increase the frequency with which a rat stands on its hind legs by making the presentation of water contingent upon that response?

☐ yes
☐ no

yes

- -

55

Stimuli that are reinforcing for individuals of one species:

    ☐ must be

    ☐ need not be

reinforcing for individuals of another species.

But if a stimulus is a reinforcer for one response that an individual organism makes, it can be a reinforcer for:

    ☐ many other responses

    ☐ no other responses

- -

need not be

many other responses

O-3

The Principle of Reinforcement

1

To determine whether or not a particular stimulus event acts as a reinforcer for a given organism, we must:

1. Select an operant response that the organism can perform.
2. Observe the rate prior to conditioning. To do this, we would first measure the _____ _____ of that response.

operant level

2

After determining the operant level, we would establish a contingency between two events. What are the two events?

1. _____

2. _____

1. the response (we have selected)

2. the stimulus (whose reinforcing power we are testing)

DRAW the paradigm for this contingency. (REMEMBER: We don't know yet whether our stimulus is a reinforcer.)

$R \longrightarrow S$

3

Here is our contingency:

$$R \longrightarrow S$$

One aspect of the contingency is *not* stated in any obvious way in the paradigm. This aspect has to do with the *time* between the stimulus and the response.

STATE this necessary feature. _____

> The stimulus must *immediately* follow the response.
> (or equivalent answer)

- -

4

What must happen before we can present the stimulus we are testing? (HINT: We may have to wait a while before it happens.) _____

> The organism must respond.
> (or equivalent answer)

- -

5

The contingency we have set up provides that
_____.

> each time the response occurs it is followed immediately by the stimulus we are testing
> (or equivalent answer)

- -

6

To determine whether or not our stimulus is a reinforcer, we observe whether or not _____.

> there is an increase in the rate of the response
> (or equivalent answer)

- -

7

In the cumulative records below, the arrow indicates the moment at which the contingency begins to be applied.

Which of the following records shows evidence that our stimulus *is* a reinforcer?

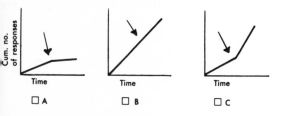

☐ A   ☐ B   ☐ C

C

8

If a record such as the one pictured is obtained, we know that the stimulus which we are testing is a(n) _____. Our paradigm, $R \longrightarrow S$, can now be written as follows:

reinforcer *or* reinforcing stimulus *or* S^R

$R \longrightarrow S^R$

9

$R \longrightarrow S^R$

Using a particular response, we have established that our stimulus was a reinforcer.

Did we say what particular response was chosen?

☐ yes   ☐ no

no

10

In reflex conditioning, the *form* of the response—
its physical description—is determined by the:

- ☐ nature of the eliciting stimulus
- ☐ requirements for producing the reinforcement

In operant conditioning, the form of the response
is determined by the:

- ☐ nature of the eliciting stimulus
- ☐ requirements for producing the reinforcement

— — — — — — — — — — — — — — — — — — —

nature of the eliciting
stimulus

requirements for produc-
ing the reinforcement

11

A

Some responses are affected only by stimuli which precede them.

B

Some responses are affected by the consequences they produce in the environment.

1. A bell elicits pupil contraction.

2. A dog sat up and received a biscuit.

3. Hearing the refrigerator door open made her mouth water.

4. He spelled the word correctly and won first prize.

Of the above, which are examples of *A* and which of *B*?

	A	B
1.	☐	☐
2.	☐	☐
3.	☐	☐
4.	☐	☐

Which are conditioned reflexes and which are conditioned operants?

	Conditioned Reflexes	Conditioned Operants
1.	☐	☐
2.	☐	☐
3.	☐	☐
4.	☐	☐

	A	B
1.	☒	☐
2.	☐	☒
3.	☒	☐
4.	☐	☒

	Conditioned Reflexes	Conditioned Operants
1.	☒	☐
2.	☐	☒
3.	☒	☐
4.	☐	☒

12

NOTE

You may have noticed that the two kinds of conditioning we have described differ in the kinds of
responses conditioned. Responses performed by the
smooth muscles, glands, and cardiac muscle are
under the control of a specific part of the nervous
system called the *autonomic* system. Behavior exe-
cuted by the skeletal (or striped or striate) muscula-
ture is under the control of a different part of the
nervous system called the *somatic* system.

NO RESPONSE REQUIRED

NO RESPONSE REQUIRED;
GO ON TO NEXT FRAME

- -

13

The following questions refer to the two types of responses listed below:

Autonomic Responses (smooth muscle, gland, and cardiac muscle responses)	*Somatic Responses* (skeletal muscle responses)
pupil dilation	standing straight
heart beat	walking
salivation	talking
"goose bumps"	hitting a ball
eyes watering	pressing a lever

(CHECK your answers after each question.)

a. Which responses can be conditioned by using the reflex conditioning procedure?

☐ autonomic

☐ somatic

autonomic

b. What procedure is used to condition the somatic responses? _____ _____

operant conditioning

c. If you observed a skeletal muscle response, you might assume it could be conditioned by using a(n):

☐ operant conditioning procedure

☐ reflex conditioning procedure

operant conditioning procedure

d. A reflex conditioning procedure must be used in conditioning:

☐ glandular responses

☐ somatic responses

☐ cardiac responses

glandular responses

cardiac responses

e. If you want to condition a somatic response, you would (☐ elicit ☐ reinforce) that response.

reinforce

f. In selecting a response for operant conditioning, you would choose a(n):

☐ autonomic response

☐ skeletal response

skeletal response

14

There is nothing special about bar-pressing, key-pecking, or operating telegraph keys. In our operant conditioning experiments with rats, pigeons, monkeys, and children, we could have chosen:

☐ any autonomic response

☐ any somatic response

any somatic response

- -

15

In operant conditioning, we identified a given stimulus as reinforcing by using it to increase the _____ of responding.

rate

Suppose that we choose a second operant response, different from the first. Could we use our reinforcer to condition this *other* response too (in the same organism)? ☐ yes ☐ no

yes

- -

16

It follows that the principle of operant conditioning applies to:

☐ a great variety of behaviors

a great variety of behaviors

☐ highly specific responses

- -

17

Once we have identified a reinforcer for a given organism, we can use it to reinforce any _____ that that organism can perform.

operant *or* somatic response

- -

18

Somatic, or skeletal, responses are strengthened through the procedure known as _____ conditioning.

operant

- -

19

With reinforcers such as food or water, the likelihood that we can strengthen operant responses in any member of the species is:

☐ high
☐ low

high

_ _

20

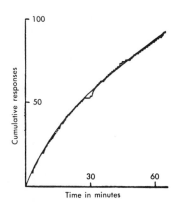

The figure shows a cumulative response curve for a rat whose bar-presses were reinforced with pellets of food. (A smoothed curve has been fitted to the response record.)

At the end of 30 minutes, the rat had made:

☐ fewer than 50 responses
☐ more than 50 responses

more than 50 responses

At the end of 60 minutes, the total number of responses was:

☐ fewer than 100
☐ more than 100

fewer than 100

Inspection of the curve shows the response rate to be:

☐ increasing
☐ decreasing

decreasing

_ _

21

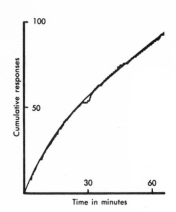

As times goes by, response rate is decreasing.

The rat is being reinforced with a pellet of food after each response.

What is the rat doing between responses? _____

eating *or* eating food pellets
(or equivalent answer)

- -

22

As the animal continues to respond and eat pellets, his rate of responding is:

☐ increasing
☐ decreasing

decreasing

- -

23

The greater the amount of food the animal has eaten, the (☐ higher ☐ lower) is his rate of responding.

lower

The relationship between previous number of pellets eaten and rate of response is:

☐ direct
☐ inverse

inverse

- -

24

If we plotted a graph of the relationship between number of pellets previously eaten and response rate, would the relationship resemble Graph *A* or Graph *B*?

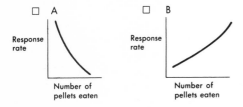

B

– –

25

Suppose we had two rats. Rat A is fed just before our experiment; rat B is deprived of food. In both cases, bar-pressing produces a pellet of food. Which rat would you expect to show the higher response rate?

☐ rat A
☐ rat B

rat B

– –

26

A rat who has just "eaten his fill" is called satiated. Which rat gave the higher response rate when bar-pressing produced food?

☐ the deprived rat
☐ the satiated rat

the deprived rat

– –

27

A given stimulus will be most effective as a reinforcer if the organism is:

☐ deprived with respect to that stimulus

☐ satiated with respect to that stimulus

deprived with respect to that stimulus

– –

28

If a rat is not responding in our experiment because he is satiated, we can increase the response rate if we _____ him of food.

deprive

29

If the organism is satiated, the reinforcing stimulus:

☐ may not be effective in strengthening behavior

☐ will still be effective in strengthening behavior

may not be effective in strengthening behavior

30

For a positive reinforcer (such as food) to be effective in strengthening behavior, the organism must be:

☐ deprived (of that reinforcer)

☐ satiated (for that reinforcer)

deprived (of that reinforcer)

31

A rat is in an experimental box with a lever in it. He is not pressing the lever. How shall we interpret this?

☐ He was never conditioned.

☐ He *was* conditioned, but is satiated.

☐ Both interpretations are possible.

Both interpretations are possible.

32

If we don't know the rat's history, how can we determine whether he was never conditioned, or whether he *was* conditioned but is now satiated?

We could _____ him of food.

deprive

33

If we deprive the rat of food, we can tell whether he has been conditioned or not. If he has been conditioned, he will _____.

respond
(or equivalent answer)

34

We have been talking about food as a reinforcer for operant behavior. In studying reflex behavior, we used food also. It was a:

☐ CS
☐ US

US

35

When used as a *US*, the food:

☐ preceded the response
☐ followed the response

preceded the response

When used as an S^R, food:

☐ preceded the response
☐ followed the response

followed the response

36

The food used as a *US* in a salivary reflex is:

☐ a different stimulus from the food used in operant conditioning
☐ the same stimulus as in operant conditioning, but used in a different way

the same stimulus as in operant conditioning, but used in a different way

---

37

Some stimuli—like food—can be used in two ways. When a stimulus elicits a response (such as salivation):

☐ it precedes the response in time

☐ it follows the response in time

When it strengthens operant behavior, the stimulus:

☐ precedes the response in time

☐ follows the response in time

it precedes the response in time

follows the response in time

38

$US \longrightarrow R$

$CS \dashrightarrow$

$R \longrightarrow S^R$

Ⓐ   Ⓑ

What symbol stands for the food in paradigm A? _____

In paradigm B? _____

US

S^R

39

$US \longrightarrow R$ $R \longrightarrow S^R$

$CS \dashrightarrow$

Reflex   Operant

Food can be used to strengthen a response, as in _____ conditioning.

It can also be used to make a new stimulus effective, as in _____ conditioning.

operant

reflex

40

You may have noticed that Pavlov's (and Anrep's) experiments employed "a hungry dog."

For the food to elicit a strong salivary response, the dog had to be:
- ☐ deprived
- ☐ satiated

deprived

- -

41

Reflex and operant conditioning both depend upon the power of certain stimuli. Through pairing, neutral stimuli can come to elicit behavior (in _____ conditioning).

reflex

The presentation of a reinforcing stimulus following a response can increase the strength of the response (in _____ conditioning).

operant

- -

42

A given stimulus:
- ☐ can be used to condition new responses in the same organism
- ☐ may be effective for other members of the same species
- ☐ may be effective for members of different species
- ☐ depends on deprivation for its effectiveness
- ☐ may act as a US or an S^R
- ☐ may be replaced by a previously neutral stimulus after conditioning

ALL are correct.

O-4

Escape Conditioning

1

PREVIEW FRAME

Thus far we have dealt with reflex conditioning, and one type of operant conditioning.

The following section will introduce you to another type of operant conditioning.

NO RESPONSE REQUIRED

NO RESPONSE REQUIRED; GO ON TO NEXT FRAME

2

An aversive noise is one from which we would tend to turn away or otherwise escape.

We can reduce the effect of or escape from an aversive noise by putting our hands over our ears.

The behavior here is called *escape behavior*.

The stimulus here is _____.

The response is _____.

The effect of the response is:
- ☐ to escape from the noise
- ☐ to increase the noise

(aversive) noise

putting hands over ears (or equivalent answer)

to escape from the noise

3

If we reduce the effect of an aversive noise by putting our hands over our ears, our behavior is called _____ behavior.

escape

4

By turning off an aversive light, we can escape from it.

NUMBER the following in the order in which they occur:

_____ bright light on

_____ bright light off

_____ escape response

1

3

2

- - - - - - - - - - - - - - - - - - - -

5

If a noise is one from which we would try to escape, it is called a(n) _____ stimulus.

Our response to this kind of stimulus is called _____.

aversive

escape behavior

- - - - - - - - - - - - - - - - - - - -

6

Now let us turn back to the laboratory situation.

We place a rat in a free-operant apparatus, and administer an electric shock through the metal cage floor. When the rat presses the bar, the shock goes off for two seconds.

What is the aversive stimulus? _____

What is the response? _____

What is the effect of the response? _____

shock

bar-press

shock goes off
(or equivalent answer)

- - - - - - - - - - - - - - - - - - - -

7

The escape response is followed by:

☐ continuation of the shock

☐ removal of the shock

Which is reinforcing?

☐ presentation of the shock

☐ removal of the shock

☐ the shock itself

removal of the shock

removal of the shock

- - - - - - - - - - - - - - - - - - - -

8

If, in the presence of the shock, the rat presses the bar, what happens to the shock? _____

                        It goes off. (or equivalent answer)

In escape conditioning, the reinforcement:
- ☐ precedes the operant response
- ☐ follows the operant response

                        follows the operant response

In the type of operant conditioning we studied previously, the reinforcement:
- ☐ preceded the operant response
- ☐ followed the operant response

                        followed the operant response

- -

9

For escape conditioning to take place, must the animal respond in the presence of the shock?
- ☐ yes
- ☐ no

                        yes

If he responds, and the response is followed by removal of shock, the strength of the behavior:
- ☐ will decrease
- ☐ will increase

                        will increase

- -

10

In escape conditioning, does the mere presence of the shock increase the frequency of the bar-press response?
- ☐ yes
- ☐ no

                        no

What does increase the rate of responding?
_____

                        removal of the shock (or equivalent answer)

- -

11

Can we say that the shock reinforces the escape response?

    ☐ yes

    ☐ no

What is the reinforcement for the escape response?

_____

no

The removal of shock is the reinforcement. (or equivalent answer)

12

Now STATE the contingency (between the response and the reinforcement) in escape conditioning for the example we have been discussing.

_____

Bar-press is followed by the removal of shock. (or equivalent answer)

13

Another way to state the contingency is:

    In the presence of shock, the bar-press response terminates _____.

shock *or* the shock

14

Now LOOK at this diagram:

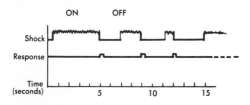

During the first 5 seconds, is the shock present?

☐ yes

☐ no

When the bar-press occurred, what happened to the shock? _____

15

Below is a diagram in which the shock and the response lines are missing. Assuming that the shock is turned on at 1 second, and that the rat presses the bar at 7 seconds, DRAW the stimulus and response lines to show what happens to the shock:

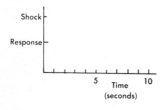

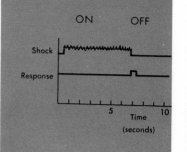

16

Which of the following is reinforcing?

    ☐ presentation of an aversive stimulus

    ☐ removal of the aversive stimulus

    ☐ the aversive stimulus

- -

removal of the aversive stimulus

17

In escape conditioning:

    The removal of an aversive stimulus is
    _____.

    Stimulus removal is contingent upon
    _____.

If the removal of a stimulus strengthens the preceding behavior, we call the stimulus a(n) _____ stimulus.

- -

reinforcing

a response *or* responding

aversive

18

We now have two types of operant conditioning which increase response strength:

    1. Presentation of a stimulus is contingent upon the response.
    2. Removal of a stimulus is contingent upon the response.

Which type of operant conditioning listed above describes the experiment in which food was used to strengthen bar-pressing? ☐ 1 ☐ 2

Which type describes the experiment in which shock was used to strengthen bar-pressing?
☐ 1 ☐ 2

- -

1

2

19

1. Presentation of food is contingent upon bar-pressing.
2. Removal of shock is contingent upon bar-pressing.

In comparing the two procedures, we see that the response was:

□ the same

□ different

                    the same

and the stimuli are:

□ the same

□ different

                    different

Which procedure describes escape conditioning?
□ 1   □ 2

                    2

- -

20

We say that for a deprived rat, water is a *positive* reinforcing stimulus.

We say that an intense shock is a *negative* reinforcing stimulus.

If a response which removes a stimulus is increased in rate, that stimulus is a:

□ negative reinforcing stimulus

                    negative reinforcing stimulus

□ positive reinforcing stimulus

- -

21

Removal of shock is contingent upon the bar-press response.

What is the negative reinforcing stimulus?

_____

                    shock

What is the reinforcement for the bar-press response? _____

                    removal of the shock

- -

22

A negative reinforcing stimulus is one from which an animal tries to escape. It is also called a(n) _____ stimulus.

aversive

- -

23

An increase in response strength occurs when a positive reinforcing stimulus is:

☐ presented after a response

☐ terminated or removed after a response

and when a negative reinforcing stimulus is:

☐ presented after a response

☐ terminated or removed after a response

presented after a response

terminated or removed after a response

- -

24

COMPLETE these statements:

Response strength increases when a response is followed by the presentation of a(n) _____.

positive reinforcing stimulus

Response strength increases when a response is followed by the removal of a(n) _____.

negative reinforcing stimulus *or* aversive stimulus

- -

25

In the blank following each of the following examples, WRITE the letter "P" or "N" to indicate whether the stimulus is positive or negative:

A man closes the window and shuts out the sound of a neighbor's record player. _____

A man goes to a theater and sees a movie. _____

A rat presses a bar and gets water. _____

A woman pulls a curtain and thus keeps the sun out. _____

N

P

P

N

26

When the removal of a negative reinforcing stimulus is contingent upon a response, what is the reinforcement? _____

removal of the (negative reinforcing) stimulus

When the presentation of a positive reinforcing stimulus is contingent upon a response, what is the reinforcement? _____

presentation of the (positive reinforcing) stimulus

27

If the experimenter is using negative reinforcement, he presents a stimulus before a response. In what other conditioning procedure that you are familiar with does the stimulus precede the response? _____

reflex conditioning

28

In both reflex conditioning and operant escape conditioning, a stimulus is presented:

☐ before a response occurs
☐ after a response occurs

before a response occurs

29

In reflex conditioning, the presentation or the termination of the stimulus (□ is produced by the response □ is not produced by the response).

is not produced by the response

30

The reflex response of an animal neither produces nor removes the _____ which controls it.

stimulus

31

However, in the operant escape situation, the aversive stimulus is _____ by the response.

terminated *or* removed (or equivalent answer)

32

In the escape situation, the response (□ affects the controlling stimulus □ does not affect the controlling stimulus).

affects the controlling stimulus

33

A similarity in the procedures for reflex and escape conditioning is that in both procedures _____.

the stimulus precedes the response (or equivalent answer)

34

But there is an important *dissimilarity*. In only one case does the response produce a change in the stimulus.

Which case is it?

☐ escape conditioning
☐ reflex conditioning

escape conditioning

35

In the escape situation, the animal operates upon the environment and thereby changes it. Escape behavior, therefore, is correctly classified as:

☐ operant behavior
☐ reflex behavior

operant behavior

36

Operant conditioning procedures using positive or negative reinforcements are alike, for, under both procedures, the animal _____ upon the environment and thereby produces a change in it.

operates *or* acts

37

REVIEW FRAME

In reflex conditioning, the stimulus precedes the response. A common measure of response strength is the time between stimulus and response. This dependent variable is called _____.

latency

38

In one operant conditioning procedure, the stimulus precedes the response. What is that procedure called? _____

escape conditioning

39

In escape conditioning we can easily measure the time between stimulus and response. A possible dependent variable in escape conditioning is, therefore, _____.

latency

40

After exposure to many trials of escape conditioning, when the aversive stimulus is presented, the escape response will occur with:

☐ long latency
☐ short latency

short latency

One evidence of strong aversive conditioning is that the response occurs with a short _____.

latency

41

The minus sign $(-)$ is commonly used to mean "negative."

If the symbol S^R stands for a positive reinforcing stimulus, you can guess that the symbol S^{-R} stands for a _____ _____ _____.

negative reinforcing stimulus

42

In order for an S^{-R} to increase response strength, it must be _____.

removed *or* terminated

In order for an S^R to increase response strength, it must be _____.

presented

43

$$\begin{bmatrix} S^{-R} \\ R \xrightarrow{\hspace{2cm}} S\!\!\!\!/^{R} \end{bmatrix}$$

In the paradigm above, the *bracket* stands for the words "in the presence of," and the *slash* stands for the word "terminates" or "removes."

STATE the paradigm as a sentence.

_____

This is the paradigm for:
    ☐ escape conditioning
    ☐ reflex conditioning

escape conditioning

— — — — — — — — — — — — — — — — — — —

44

On a very hot day, we have the air conditioner turned on. The air conditioner occasionally does not function properly, but we can fix it by hitting the top of it with our fist.

With "heat" as the aversive stimulus, DIAGRAM the contingency in this example:

$$\begin{bmatrix} S^{-R} \\ (\hspace{1cm}) \\ R \xrightarrow{\hspace{2cm}} S\!\!\!\!/^{R} \\ (\hspace{1cm}) \; (\hspace{1cm}) \end{bmatrix}$$

$$\begin{bmatrix} S^{-R} \\ (\text{heat}) \\ R \xrightarrow{\hspace{2cm}} S\!\!\!\!/^{R} \\ (\text{hitting}) \hspace{1.5cm} (\text{heat}) \end{bmatrix}$$

— — — — — — — — — — — — — — — — — — —

45

DIAGRAM the escape conditioning contingency.

— — — — — — — — — — — — — — — — — — —

46

$$R \longrightarrow S^R$$

The paradigm above means that the S^R is:

☐ presented

☐ removed

$$\begin{bmatrix} S^{-R} \\ R \longrightarrow S^{-R} \end{bmatrix}$$

The paradigm above means that the S^{-R} is:

☐ presented

☐ removed

☐ presented, then removed

— — — — — — — — — — — — — — — — — — — —

47

$$R \longrightarrow S^R$$

STATE the events implied by the paradigm above.

_____

In this paradigm, we imply that the positive reinforcing stimulus is:

☐ presented

☐ removed

— — — — — — — — — — — — — — — — — — — —

presented

presented, then removed

The response is followed by a positive reinforcing stimulus.
(or equivalent answer)

presented

48

1. $R \longrightarrow S^R$

2. $\begin{bmatrix} S^{-R} \\ R \longrightarrow \cancel{S^{-R}} \end{bmatrix}$

What is the reinforcing *event* in each contingency?

1. _____

2. _____

the *presentation* of the positive reinforcing stimulus

the *removal* of the negative reinforcing stimulus (or equivalent answers)

– –

49

WRITE the two paradigms for the operant conditioning contingencies that increase response rate and STATE specifically what each one means: (LABEL the paradigm for escape conditioning with the letter "E.")

1.

2.

$R \longrightarrow S^R$

A response is followed by the *presentation* of a positive reinforcing stimulus.

$\begin{bmatrix} S^{-R} \\ R \longrightarrow \cancel{S^{-R}} \end{bmatrix}$ Ⓔ

In the presence of a negative reinforcing stimulus, a response is followed by the *removal* of the stimulus.

– –

50

Given a stimulus, what steps would you go through to determine whether or not it was a negative reinforcing stimulus? _____

1. present the stimulus to an organism
2. remove the stimulus whenever a certain kind of response occurred
3. note whether the strength of that particular behavior increases

(or equivalent answers)

51

FOOTNOTE FRAME

We have dealt with two ways in which stimuli affect operant behavior.

As you may have supposed, there are other cases to deal with. In the two cases dealt with so far in this program, rate of responding increases when we present a positive reinforcing stimulus or terminate a negative reinforcing stimulus.

The other two cases are:

1. The *removal of a positive reinforcing stimulus* is contingent upon a response.
2. The *presentation of a negative reinforcing stimulus* is contingent upon a response.

These last two cases are called *punishment*, and the result of the contingencies may be a decrease in the rate of responding, but these cases present other complexities and will not be discussed here.

O-5

The Shaping of Behavior

1

The pigeon, when it first enters the experimental apparatus, has an operant level of zero for the key-peck response.

That is, prior to conditioning, the pigeon (□ does □ does not) emit the response.

does not

- -

2

We plan to use grain as a reinforcer. What must we do to the pigeon before the experiment to ensure that grain will be effective as a reinforcer?

_____

deprive the pigeon of grain
(or equivalent answer)

- -

3

The next step in the procedure is to familiarize the bird with the food aperture. This is easily done by leaving the food tray in position until the pigeon finds it. After he has eaten for a few seconds, it is removed. It is then presented repeatedly until the pigeon immediately goes to the hopper and eats as soon as he hears the aperture open.

This provides the means for the experimenter to present the bird with food whenever he chooses to do so; that is, the experimenter can _____ a given response as soon as it occurs.

reinforce

- -

4

Here are some examples of operant responses. Which would you guess have an operant level of zero prior to conditioning?

☐ 1. key-pecking (pigeon)
☐ 2. wing-flapping (pigeon)
☐ 3. writing (human)
☐ 4. crying (human)
☐ 5. barking (dog)
☐ 6. sitting-up (dog)
☐ 7. saying "onomatopoeia" (human)
☐ 8. jumping through a hoop (lion)
☐ 9. scratching (dog)
☐ 10. playing polo (human)

1

3

6
7
8

10

— — — — — — — — — — — — — — — — — — — —

5

The pigeon moves around the apparatus.
The dog sits down, stands up, and lies down.
The child makes many different sounds.

Above are some examples of the:
☐ stereotypy (lack of variability) of behavior
☐ variability of behavior

variability of behavior

— — — — — — — — — — — — — — — — — — — —

6

Any organism that is awake and functioning will display behavior.

For example, the pigeon in the apparatus might flap his wings, peck at the floor, move around, etc.

Over a period of time, he would display:
☐ few responses
☐ many different responses

many different responses

We can say, then, that his behavior:
☐ displays variability
☐ does not display variability

displays variability

— — — — — — — — — — — — — — — — — — — —

7

You, the experimenter, want eventually to condition a key-pecking response. Before you can begin reinforcing this response:

☐ it must occur

☐ it need not occur

it must occur

At what operant level is the key-pecking response prior to the conditioning procedure? _____

0 *or* zero

— —

8

There are three facts, then, that we must consider:

1. The behavior of the pigeon is variable.
2. The key-pecking response has an operant level of zero.
3. Behavior must be emitted in order to be reinforced.

Which of the statements below should also be considered?

☐ Some of the pigeon's varied behavior will be in the direction of the key.

Some of the pigeon's varied behavior will be in the direction of the key.

☐ It would be inefficient to wait for the pigeon to emit a response that has an operant level of zero.

It would be inefficient to wait for the pigeon to emit a response that has an operant level of zero.

— —

9

Suppose that the pigeon in the apparatus first turns away from the key and then turns toward the key. Which response should you reinforce?

☐ turning away from the key

☐ turning toward the key

turning toward the key

— —

10

If the bird turns toward the key, how soon should the experimenter deliver the reinforcement?
_____

What would be the result of this reinforcement?
_____

immediately

The frequency of turning toward the key would increase.
(or equivalent answers)

— — — — — — — — — — — — — — — — — —

11

As we reinforce turning toward the key, we might expect that the pigeon's behavior would:
- ☐ remain identical from one response to the next
- ☐ vary from one response to the next

vary from one response to the next

— — — — — — — — — — — — — — — — — —

12

The pigeon's response of turning toward the key varies each time it is made. As the experiment continues, we become more selective in the responses we reinforce. We would begin to reinforce variations which bring the animal:
- ☐ closer to the key than previous responses

- ☐ farther from the key than previous responses

closer to the key than previous responses

— — — — — — — — — — — — — — — — — —

13

If at this point we decided to wait until the pigeon pecked the key, we might have to wait a very long time, if not forever, because the operant level of key-pecking is still _____.

0 *or* zero

Therefore, we should continue to reinforce the responses that are leading the pigeon _____.

closer to the key
(or equivalent answer)

_ _

14

By reinforcing responses which bring the pigeon closer to the key, we reach the point at which (1) the pigeon has been reinforced several times for standing with his head close enough to the key to be able to reach out and peck it; and (2) he returns often to this position after reinforcement. To what part of the pigeon should we now turn our attention? _____

the head

_ _

15

We should reinforce those movements of the head in which the pigeon moves his bill _____.

closer to the key
(or equivalent answer)

_ _

16

After some reinforcement of bill movements, the pigeon's closer responses will be an approximation of the final response we set out to produce.

What is that response? _____

key-pecking *or* pecking the key

_ _

17

We have "shaped out" the response of key-pecking by:

☐ reinforcing closer and closer approximations to the final response

☐ waiting for a key peck to occur and then reinforcing it

reinforcing closer and closer approximations to the final response

- -

18

Shaping out the key-pecking response might mean reinforcing the following responses, among others.

NUMBER these responses in the order in which they would probably occur and be reinforced (using "1" for the first to be reinforced, etc.):

a. _____ facing the key

b. _____ moving to a point ½ inch from the key

c. _____ moving to a point 1 inch from the key

d. _____ moving to a point 2 inches from the key

e. _____ pecking the key

f. _____ putting the beak on the key

a. 1

b. 4

c. 3

d. 2

e. 6

f. 5

- -

19

The plastic pecking key rests against a sensitive switch. A key-peck response, the final operant, is defined as a response which closes the switch.

Which of the following responses, made near the end of the experiment, would be reinforced?

☐ A light peck on the key which closes the switch.

☐ A forceful peck on the key which closes the switch.

☐ A peck on the outer edge of the key which closes the switch.

☐ A peck on the key which closes the switch as the bird flaps his wings.

All responses listed close the switch; therefore, all are reinforced.

- -

20

When we "shape out" behavior, we gradually change the requirements of the response. We call these requirements that are changed the *properties* of the response.

Examples of such properties are:

closeness to the key

facing the key

moving the head forward

force of the response

For example, when the pigeon pecks the key, the *force* of the response must be sufficient to _____.

close the switch

These are properties of a response that determine whether, at a given point in our procedure, the experimenter will _____ the response.

reinforce

- -

21

The *defining property* of a response is that aspect of the response upon which reinforcement is contingent.

In our pigeon-conditioning procedure, the defining property of the final operant response in our procedure was that the pigeon must close the switch by _____.

pecking the key, a peck on the key
(or equivalent answer)

22

An *operant class* of responses includes those responses that have the property upon which reinforcement is contingent. However, the members of an operant class may vary somewhat from each other.

Which of the following responses would belong to the operant class of key-pecking?

□ 1. pecking the bottom of the key

□ 2. pecking the food aperture

□ 3. pecking the experimenter

□ 4. pecking the key very hard

□ 5. pecking the side of the key

□ 6. pecking the top of the key

□ 7. pecking the wall ¼ inch from the key

1. pecking the bottom of the key

4. pecking the key very hard
5. pecking the side of the key
6. pecking the top of the key

23

A basketball player makes two baskets; the first bounces off the backboard, rolls around the rim, and then goes through the basket; the second goes in without even touching the rim.

A rat presses the bar first on the left side, then on the right, then with a light force, and then with a hard force. After each press he receives a pellet of food.

A dog is trained to roll over. He first rolls over quickly and then slowly. Each time he receives a pellet of food.

In the examples above, all the responses were followed by _____. However, each response differed slightly from the immediately preceding response; in other words, the responses showed some _____.

reinforcement

variability *or* variation (or equivalent answer)

What is the defining property of the operant class of responses in the first example? _____

In the second example? _____

In the third example? _____

ball goes in basket

bar-press

rolling over (or equivalent answers)

- -

24

Suppose that we wish to condition a rat to press a bar and hold it down for at least 30 seconds. This response will be reinforced with water. The rat already is conditioned to press the bar for water, but the longest the rat has ever held the bar is 2 seconds.

What is the operant level of 30-second bar presses?

_____

0 *or* zero

The defining property of the operant class of responses to be conditioned is that each bar-press be at least 30 seconds long.

Which of the following would be in this operant class?

☐ 10-second bar-press
☐ 26-second bar-press
☐ 30-second bar-press
☐ 31-second bar-press
☐ 35-second bar-press

30-second bar-press
31-second bar-press
35-second bar-press

- -

25

The property of the bar-press response that we are interested in is:

☐ duration
☐ latency
☐ magnitude

duration

- -

26

Remember: The final operant is a bar-press of at least 30 seconds duration.

The rat has been reinforced for several 2-second bar-presses. We would now begin to reinforce only those responses with a duration of:

☐ 1 second or less

☐ 1 second or more

☐ 2 seconds or less

☐ 2 seconds or more

What aspect of the defining property of the response are we changing?

☐ its duration

☐ its magnitude

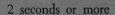

2 seconds or more

its duration

— — — — — — — — — — — — — — — — — — — —

27

Before we began reinforcing only those responses of 2 seconds or more, we had been reinforcing responses of 1 second or more.

Below is a diagram of the response class "1 second or more." DRAW in the response class that we have now adopted:

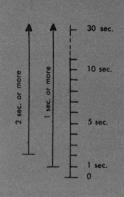

— — — — — — — — — — — — — — — — — — — —

28

By our definition of the response class, all bar-press responses that have the property of having a duration of 2 seconds or more are in:

☐ different operant classes

☐ the same operant class

the same operant class

- - - - - - - - - - - - - - - - - -

29

When we changed the property of the operant class from 1 second or more, we redefined the class. In this case, the new class has the property of _____.

a duration of 2 seconds or more
(or equivalent answer)

- - - - - - - - - - - - - - - - - -

30

As a result of reinforcing responses in the 2-second-or-more operant class, the frequency of occurrence of responses greater than 2 seconds would:

☐ decrease

☐ increase

increase

- - - - - - - - - - - - - - - - - -

31

Suppose that the defining property of the operant class is still a duration of 2 seconds or more. Which of the following would you predict would happen?

☐ The rat's behavior becomes stereotyped; almost all of his responses are of 2-second duration.

☐ The rat's behavior remains variable; there are some responses of 2-second duration, and many of longer than 2 seconds.

The rat's behavior remains variable; there are some responses of 2-second duration, and many of longer than 2 seconds.

- - - - - - - - - - - - - - - - - -

32

We are reinforcing *any* response whose duration is 2 seconds or more. The rat's behavior is (☐ fixed ☐ variable). Because of this, the rat will make some responses of 3 seconds or more. When this has occurred several times, we can again _____.

variable

redefine the operant class *or* increase the required duration
(or equivalent answer)

- -

33

During "shaping," in order to reach the terminal operant of a 30-second-long response, it is important that the rat's behavior at each stage continue to be:

    ☐ variable
    ☐ stereotyped

variable

- -

34

This variability gives us a variety of responses to select from. We select those with certain properties (similar to those of the final operant) and _____ them.

reinforce

- -

35

As the duration of responses increases, we can change the property on which reinforcement is contingent.

In other words, we can successively redefine the _____.

operant class

We will continue this until the duration of responses reaches _____ seconds.

30 (seconds)

- -

36

The operant is redefined in a successive series of:
- ☐ large steps
- ☐ small steps

Thus, we increase the required response duration:
- ☐ gradually
- ☐ sharply

small steps

gradually

- - - - - - - - - - - - - - - - - - - -

37

Our end result should be a 30-second bar-press if we successively redefine the properties of the reinforced response. By our successive redefinitions of the properties of the response, the operant class:
- ☐ was changed
- ☐ remained the same

An operant class is a set of responses that have _____.

was changed

a common property
(or equivalent answer)

- - - - - - - - - - - - - - - - - - - -

38

We shape an entirely new response by successively _____ the operant class.

This is done in (☐ large ☐ small) steps.

An operant class is a set of responses that have a common _____ upon which _____ is contingent.

redefining

small

property
reinforcement

- - - - - - - - - - - - - - - - - - - -

39

You are asked to shape a chain-pulling response in a rat. (A small metal chain connected to a switch hangs from the ceiling of the cage.) Assume that the rat is thirsty and has been shaped to go to the dipper and drink when the dipper sound occurs.

The operant level of the chain-pulling response is zero, so your task is to condition (□ an existing response □ a new response).

LIST in order at least six operants that you would reinforce in shaping this response:

1.

2.

3.

4.

5.

6. pulling the chain

a new response

SAMPLE ANSWER
1. any response of facing the chain

2. slight movements toward the chain (small steps)

3. touching the chain

4. any response in which the rat stands up, still touching the chain

5. grabbing the chain while standing on hind legs

6. (pulling the chain)

Your answer should illustrate a procedure for redefining the operant:
   in small steps
   in the direction of the desired response

40

DEFINE an operant class.

_____

An operant class is composed of responses that have a common property. (or equivalent answer)

- -

41

We develop new behavior by making _____ contingent upon gradual changes in the common _____ which defines the _____

_____

reinforcement

property   operant class

The procedure you have been studying here is called *shaping*. Behavior can be shaped by redefining the _____ in _____ steps.

operant class   small

Shaping is an appropriate name for this procedure because it:

☐ changes the form of behavior

☐ changes the form of the stimuli

changes the form of behavior

- -

42

If we wish to condition an entirely new response, we would use a procedure called _____. In order to do this, the operant class is _____ in _____ steps.

shaping
redefined
small

- -

43

Humans learn to:

    speak languages

    play basketball

    walk tightropes

    adjust watches

In all these cases, the behavior required is:

    ☐ present at birth

    ☐ not present at birth

Such behavior:

    ☐ has a substantial operant level before conditioning

    ☐ has a very low or zero operant level before conditioning

    ☐ needs to be developed through a series of gradual approximations (in small steps)

> not present at birth
>
> has a very low or zero operant level before conditioning
>
> needs to be developed through a series of gradual approximations ·(in small steps)

- -

44

The process of developing these complex forms of behavior in small steps is called _____.

> shaping

- -

45

The process of shaping makes possible the creation of new _____.

> responses *or* (operant) behavior

- -

Review: Reflexes and Operants in the Behaving Organism

1

In Pavlov's experiments, a conditioning procedure was used to make a tone produce salivation.

The stimulus which originally *did* produce salivation was called the _____ stimulus.

unconditioned

- -

2

The tone was originally called a neutral stimulus. Why was this stimulus called "neutral"?

_____

It did not produce salivation.
(or equivalent answer)

- -

3

After conditioning, the tone came to elicit salivation. This new stimulus-response relationship was called a(n) _____ reflex.

conditioned

- -

4

The procedure required to produce a conditioned reflex involved repeated pairings of the _____ stimulus and the _____ stimulus.

conditioned *or* neutral
unconditioned

- -

5

DRAW the paradigm for the conditioning procedure developed by Pavlov:

$$US \longrightarrow R$$
$$CS \dashrightarrow R$$

- -

6

$$US \longrightarrow R$$

The paradigm above represents an unconditioned reflex.

First the ＿＿ (symbol) is presented.

Then the ＿＿ (symbol) occurs.

US

R

- -

7

$$CS \longrightarrow R$$

The paradigm above represents a conditioned reflex.

First event: ＿＿

Second event: ＿＿

CS (presented)

R (occurs)

- -

8

For both conditioned and unconditioned reflexes, the ＿＿ precedes the ＿＿.

$$S \longrightarrow R$$
(stimulus)   (response)

- -

9

To condition a reflex, we pair two stimuli. For most effective conditioning, which usually comes first?

☐ US

☐ neutral stimulus

The neutral stimulus becomes a(n) ＿＿＿＿＿＿＿.

neutral stimulus

CS *or* conditioned stimulus

- -

10

$$R \longrightarrow S$$

Operant behavior produces effects.

Which occurs first?

☐ behavior

☐ effects

Then comes:

☐ behavior

☐ effects

behavior

effects

11

$$R \longrightarrow S$$

In the operant paradigm above, the arrow
($\longrightarrow$) is read:

☐ "elicits"

☐ "is followed by"

"is followed by"

12

$$S \longrightarrow R$$

In the reflex paradigm above, the arrow is read
_____.

"elicits"

13

If an operant response is followed by a reinforcing stimulus, the strength of the response will:

☐ increase

☐ decrease

increase

14

When a stimulus is effective in increasing the
strength of an operant response, our paradigm
$R \longrightarrow S$ becomes _____. (DRAW
the paradigm.)

$$R \longrightarrow S^R$$

15

In Pavlovian conditioning, the eliciting stimulus occurs:

    ☐ before the response

    ☐ after the response

In operant conditioning, the positive reinforcing stimulus occurs:

    ☐ before the response

    ☐ after the response

before the response

after the response

- -

16

$$\begin{bmatrix} S^{-R} \\ R \longrightarrow \cancel{S}^{\leftarrow R} \end{bmatrix}$$

In escape conditioning, an aversive stimulus is present. The effect of the response is to _____ that stimulus.

terminate *or* remove

- -

17

In escape conditioning, another name for the aversive stimulus is the _____ reinforcing stimulus.

negative

- -

18

What is the reinforcement in escape conditioning?

_____

termination of the aversive stimulus *or* termination of the negative reinforcing stimulus

- -

19

In escape conditioning, the reinforcement (☐ precedes ☐ follows) the response.

follows

- -

20

Escape conditioning is an example of:
- ☐ operant conditioning
- ☐ Pavlovian conditioning

operant conditioning

- -

21

The response precedes the reinforcement in _____ conditioning.

operant

- -

22

The *US* precedes the response in _____ conditioning.

reflex *or* Pavlovian

- -

23

The response is elicited by a specific stimulus in:
- ☐ operant conditioning
- ☐ reflex conditioning

reflex conditioning

The response produces the reinforcement in:
- ☐ operant conditioning
- ☐ reflex conditioning

operant conditioning

- -

24

To control reflex behavior, we must present a(n) _____.

stimulus

To strengthen operant behavior, we must wait for a(n) _____.

response

- -

25

a. The response operates upon the environment to produce consequences. This is:

    ☐ operant behavior

    ☐ reflex behavior

b. The stimulus produces (elicits) the response. This is:

    ☐ operant behavior

    ☐ reflex behavior

Which of the statements above illustrates escape behavior?

    ☐ *a.*

    ☐ *b.*

operant behavior

reflex behavior

a.

- -

26

The terms "simultaneous," "delay," and "trace" refer to different time relationships between two
_____.

These terms apply to:

    ☐ operant conditioning

    ☐ Pavlovian conditioning

stimuli

Pavlovian conditioning

- -

27

In Pavlovian conditioning, the term "latency" refers to the time lapse between a(n) _____ and a(n) _____.

Latency is:

    ☐ a dependent variable

    ☐ an independent variable

stimulus
response

a dependent variable

- -

28

In Pavlovian conditioning, the experimenter can choose any value he pleases for:

☐ the time interval between two stimuli
☐ the time interval between stimulus and response

the time interval between two stimuli

- -

29

The significant time relationship in operant conditioning is the time between a(n) _____ and the _____ that follows it.

response
stimulus

- -

30

For effective operant conditioning, the reinforcement must occur _____ after the response.

immediately

- -

31

The time interval between stimuli is up to the experimenter in:

☐ operant conditioning
☐ Pavlovian conditioning

Pavlovian conditioning

The time interval between a response and a reinforcement is determined by the experimenter in:

☐ operant conditioning
☐ Pavlovian conditioning

operant conditioning

- -

32

In Pavlovian conditioning, two stimuli are paired. A neutral stimulus is paired with a(n) _____, and as a result the neutral stimulus becomes a(n) _____.

US *or* unconditioned stimulus
CS *or* conditioned stimulus

The new reflex gets stronger as a result of:

☐ fewer pairings
☐ more pairings

more pairings

- -

33

The number of pairings between two stimuli (in Pavlovian conditioning) is:

    ☐ a dependent variable

    ☐ an independent variable

an independent variable

34

We strengthen operant behavior by waiting for the _____, then following it with a(n) _____.

response

stimulus *or* reinforcing stimulus

We make the interval between the two:

    ☐ as long as possible

    ☐ as short as possible

as short as possible

35

After many pairings, a Pavlovian conditioned reflex is strong. We measure this by observing that latency:

    ☐ increases

    ☐ decreases

decreases

and that response magnitude:

    ☐ increases

    ☐ decreases

increases

36

Latency and magnitude are:

    ☐ dependent variables

    ☐ independent variables

dependent variables

37

In operant conditioning, as a result of a contingency between the response and the reinforcing stimulus, the rate of responding:

☐ increases
☐ decreases

increases

- -

38

As Pavlovian conditioning proceeds, the CS elicits the response with a(n) _____ latency and a(n) _____ magnitude.

shorter
greater

- -

39

In *operant* conditioning, the cumulative record shows the number of responses in a given time period. Responses per minute is called the _____ of responding.

rate

- -

40

Commonly there are *two* important measures in a Pavlovian conditioning experiment. They are:

1. _____
2. _____

latency
magnitude
(any order)

- -

41

Latency, magnitude, and rate are all examples of:
- ☐ dependent variables
- ☐ independent variables

Magnitude is increased and latency decreased by the:
- ☐ contingency between a response and a reinforcement
- ☐ pairing of a neutral and an unconditioned stimulus

dependent variables

pairing of a neutral and an unconditioned stimulus

- -

42

We increase magnitude and decrease latency by:
- ☐ pairing stimuli
- ☐ arranging a contingency between a response and a stimulus

We increase the rate of responding by:
- ☐ pairing stimuli
- ☐ arranging a contingency between a response and reinforcement

pairing stimuli

arranging a contingency between a response and reinforcement

- -

43

The procedures of *pairing stimuli* and *arranging a contingency* are both examples of:
- ☐ dependent variables
- ☐ independent variables

independent variables

- -

44

The *pairing* of stimuli is the independent variable for:

☐ operant conditioning
☐ Pavlovian conditioning

Pavlovian conditioning

The *contingency* between a response and a re-inforcement is the independent variable for:

☐ operant conditioning
☐ Pavlovian conditioning

operant conditioning

45

In operant conditioning, a dependent variable commonly employed to measure response strength is the _____ of responding.

rate

46

$$US \longrightarrow R \qquad R \longrightarrow S^R$$
$$CS \dashrightarrow$$

Reflex   *Operant*
Conditioning   *Conditioning*

In reflex conditioning, eliciting stimuli are presented to the animal regardless of what he is doing. Is this true of operant conditioning? ☐ yes
☐ no

no

47

$$US \longrightarrow R \qquad R \longrightarrow S^R$$
$$CS \dashrightarrow \qquad \begin{bmatrix} S{-}R \\ R \longrightarrow \cancel{S{-}R} \end{bmatrix}$$

In operant conditioning, what has to happen before the reinforcement occurs? _____

The response must occur.
(or equivalent answer)

48

A response produces a reinforcement by actively operating upon the environment. The procedure is called _____.

operant conditioning

- -

49

For each statement, CHECK the type(s) of conditioning to which it applies:

	TYPE OF CONDITIONING			TYPE OF CONDITIONING		
	US→R / CS⁻	R→S^R	[S^{-R} / R→S^R	US→R / CS⁻	R→S^R	[S^{-R} / R→S^R
The eliciting stimulus comes first.	☐	☐	☐	☒	☐	☐
The response precedes the reinforcement.	☐	☐	☐	☐	☒	☒
The response produces reinforcement.	☐	☐	☐	☐	☒	☒
Two stimuli are paired.	☐	☐	☐	☒	☐	☐
If a response has certain effects, it will occur more often.	☐	☐	☐	☐	☒	☒
Applies to autonomic responses (smooth muscle, cardiac muscle, glands)	☐	☐	☐	☒	☐	☐
Applies to somatic responses	☐	☐	☐	☐	☒	☒
Escape	☐	☐	☐	☐	☐	☒
Latency of response is a dependent variable.	☐	☐	☐	☒	☐	☒
Response terminates an aversive stimulus.	☐	☐	☐	☐	☐	☒
I. P. Pavlov	☐	☐	☐	☒	☐	☐
Operant Conditioning	☐	☐	☐	☐	☒	☒

- -

50

CHECK the type of conditioning that each sentence describes:

	TYPE OF CONDITIONING	
	Reflex	Operant
The response occurred at a very high rate.	☐	☐
The stimulus was too weak to elicit the response.	☐	☐
In the presence of an aversive stimulus, a response terminates that stimulus.	☐	☐
Once a response occurs, it can be reinforced.	☐	☐
After many pairings, a neutral stimulus will elicit the response.	☐	☐

- - - - - - - - - - - - - - - - - - - -

51

There are other major differences between operant and reflex conditioning. Under one procedure, a stimulus is paired with another stimulus. This takes place in _____ conditioning.

- - - - - - - - - - - - - - - - - - - -

52

In reflex conditioning, the US and CS are _____ with one another.

- - - - - - - - - - - - - - - - - - - -

53

After repeated pairings, the CS alone will _____ a response.

Thus, the CS will now *substitute* for the _____.

- - - - - - - - - - - - - - - - - - - -

54

"Stimulus substitution" means that the same or a similar response to the one following the US can be elicited by the _____.

- - - - - - - - - - - - - - - - - - - -

Answer column (shaded):

	TYPE OF CONDITIONING	
	Reflex	Operant
	☐	☒
	☒	☐
	☐	☒
	☐	☒
	☒	☐

reflex

paired

elicit

US

CS

55

Stimulus substitution applies to the procedure known as _____ conditioning.

reflex *or* Pavlovian

- -

56

In order to condition a reflex, how many stimuli are needed? _____

two

- -

57

Are two stimuli needed in the operant conditioning procedure?
 ☐ yes
 ☐ no

no

- -

58

In the case of operant conditioning:
 ☐ there is stimulus substitution
 ☐ there is no stimulus substitution

there is no stimulus substitution

- -

59

The result of reflex conditioning is:
 ☐ control by a new stimulus
 ☐ the shaping of a new response

control by a new stimulus

- -

60

In what kind of conditioning can we gradually shape out new responses?
 ☐ operant conditioning
 ☐ reflex conditioning

operant conditioning

- -

61

We can condition new operant responses (whose operant level is zero to begin with) through the process of _____.

shaping

62

MATCH words or phrases with the types of conditioning:

a. reflex conditioning

b. operant conditioning

1. _____ elicits
2. _____ S^R
3. _____ stimulus substitution
4. _____ response produces stimulus
5. _____ US
6. _____ stimulus elicits response
7. _____ escape
8. _____ new responses can be shaped

1. *a*
2. *b*
3. *a*
4. *b*
5. *a*
6. *a*
7. *b*
8. *b*

63

REVIEW FRAME

FILL IN the following table, which contrasts reflex and operant conditioning:

	REFLEX	OPERANT
a. STATE whether the response precedes or follows the stimulus in time.	_____	_____
b. STATE whether the reinforcer precedes or follows the response in time.	_____	_____
c. NAME the independent variable responsible for conditioning.	_____	_____

	REFLEX	OPERANT
a.	follows	precedes
b.	precedes	follows
c.	pairing (of stimulus)	contingency (between a response and a stimulus)

64

WRITE the paradigms for:
1. an unconditioned reflex:

2. a conditioned reflex:

3. reflex conditioning:

4. 2 paradigms for operant conditioning:
   (CIRCLE the escape paradigm.)

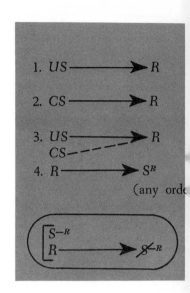

1. $US \longrightarrow R$

2. $CS \longrightarrow R$

3. $US \longrightarrow R$
   $CS \dashrightarrow$

4. $R \longrightarrow S^R$
   (any orde

   S^{-R}
   $R \longrightarrow S^{-R}$

- -

Epilogue on Operant Conditioning

by Fred S. Keller

SINCE the end of the section on *Reflexes*, you have learned quite a few things. The most obvious one, of course, is the law of operant conditioning, with which you ought now to be on intimate terms. You know its two basic forms, pictured as:

$$R \longrightarrow S^R \text{ and } \begin{bmatrix} S^{-R} \\ R \longrightarrow S^R \end{bmatrix}$$

and you have even had practice in applying this knowledge to the description of everyday human conduct.

Your understanding of human and infra-human nature has thus been greatly extended, now that you have added the basic principle of operant conditioning to Pavlov's principle of reflex conditioning. With these two principles at hand, you know the rules for setting up all kinds of responses in a wide variety of organisms, from the top of the animal scale almost to the bottom. One hundred years ago, these principles were barely glimpsed, and only within the past twenty years has their importance been fully appreciated. In fact, progress has been so rapid in this field that you yourself, at this moment, probably have a better appreciation of the "learning process" than did the *psychologists* of your parents' day.

Some matters, of course, remain to be looked after. You don't yet know, for certain, how to *weaken* behavior—either reflex or operant— once it has been conditioned. Also, you may not be able to describe the way to *maintain* conditioned behavior—how to keep response strength at a steady level throughout long periods of time. But you will find that answers to these questions rest heavily upon the two great laws that you have mastered.

213

In the section just concluded, you could have sensed the importance of the operant-conditioning *principle* without quite realizing the significance of the *method* associated with this principle. Professor Skinner's use of *rate of response,* rather than magnitude or latency, has had a great and still-growing influence upon our science; and cumulative-response curves, which portray the rate so vividly, have been produced in thousands of experiments since 1931, and studied by countless psychologists. If Pavlov's method advanced the study of the reflex and extended the psychology of learning, Skinner's method opened up an even broader realm of behavioral investigation. The entire field of "voluntary" activity, long recognized by philosophers, psychologists, and others as deserving of study, was finally drawn within the province of laboratory science. In *rate of emission* of operant behavior—the pressing of a lever, the pecking of a key, the utterance of a word, or any of a thousand other samples of non-reflex action—we were given a dependent variable that was to stir up a revolution in the study of learning and begin a new era of scientific psychology. Greater contributions are seldom made by individual workers in any branch of science.

"Operant conditioning," however, is no longer associated with the labors of just one man, and the term itself has come to mean much more than the simple strengthening of motor responses through reinforcement. A whole viewpoint in modern psychology has come to be catalogued under this heading. In addition, "operant conditioners," so-called, have made their way successfully into many practical spheres of human endeavor—e.g., into the fields of animal training, child rearing, behavior therapy, and education. (The book you are now studying is itself an attempt to apply the rules of reinforcement to the improvement of teaching procedures.) But such matters are for other volumes of this program and for other times, not for an epilogue like this.

The three books listed below were all written from the viewpoint mentioned above. All of them include some coverage of operant conditioning and its applications. Keller and Schoenfeld were the first to bring operant conditioning to the undergraduate reader ("Skinner for the beginner," one critic said!). Skinner's own, and very different, text was aimed at a similar student level; while the book by Staats and Staats, also for the first course, is a very recent attempt to show the power of the principle in the analysis of complex human learning.

These are not the only books to deal with operant conditioning, but each one, in its own way, should add to your understanding thereof.

Fred S. Keller
Professor of Psychology
University of Arizona

Keller, F. S., and Schoenfeld, W. N., *Principles of Psychology*. New York: Appleton-Century-Crofts, 1950.

Skinner, B. F., *Science and Human Behavior*. New York: Macmillan, 1953.

Staats and Staats, *Complex Behavior*. New York: Holt, Rinehart and Winston, 1963.

Editor's Note: Professor Keller has also written a short paperback book on the subject which would be an excellent addition to your library—

Keller, Fred S., *Learning (Reinforcement Theory)*. New York: Random House, 1954.

PANEL R-2-1

Pupil Contraction as a Function of Light Intensity

The experimenters, by means of an infrared photography method, were able to photograph and measure pupil contraction either in the light or in the dark. Human subjects were first kept in a darkened chamber for about 30 minutes. During the experimental session, each subject's head was held motionless by a chin rest, upright bar, and eyepiece. Successive spots of light of different intensity were flashed in the eye, and photographs of the eye taken. Each level of intensity was used several times and the results were averaged for that intensity value. In the figure below, the diameter of the pupil is plotted on the vertical axis, above the intensity (brightness) at which each observation was made.

(From: Wagman, I. H., and Nathanson, L. M., "Influence of White Light upon Pupil Diameter for the Human and for the Rabbit," in Proc. Soc. Exp. Biol. Med., 49, pp. 466-470.)

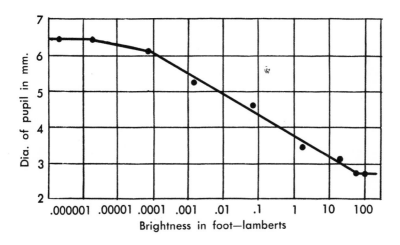

PANEL R-3-1

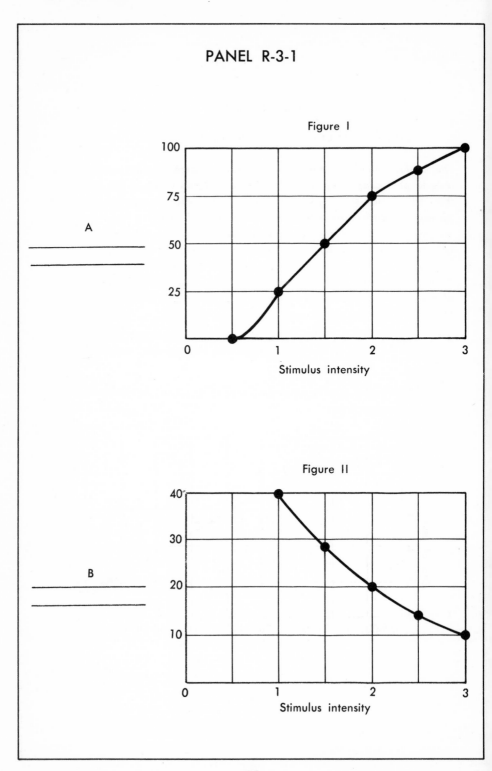

Figure I

A
_____
_____

Stimulus intensity

Figure II

B
_____
_____

Stimulus intensity

PANEL R-7-1

Ivan Pavlov (1849-1936), a Russian physiologist, was the first person to investigate the quantitative properties of conditioned reflexes in the laboratory. The following paragraphs describe one of his experiments with the salivary reflex:

Dogs served as subjects under carefully controlled laboratory conditions. The dog was placed in a harness on a table in a sound-proofed experimental room. Saliva ran from the dog's mouth into a glass measuring tube.

Session I

On several occasions food was placed in the dog's mouth. On the average the dog produced 15 drops of saliva each time food was placed in its mouth. Secretion of saliva began two seconds after introduction of the food.

Session II

With no food available, a metronome was sounded. No salivation occurred to the metronome.

Session III

The metronome was turned on. Five seconds later, food was placed in the dog's mouth. Salivation occurred 2 seconds after the food entered the dog's mouth. The metronome was turned off when the food was in the dog's mouth. This procedure was repeated 10 times. On the fifth trial three drops of saliva were produced 4 seconds after the metronome began. By the tenth repetition the dog began salivating 2 seconds after the metronome began; 10 drops were produced. Thus Pavlov successfully demonstrated conditioning of the salivary reflex.

(*Material based on descriptions in:* Pavlov, I. P., *Conditioned Reflexes.* New York: Dover Press.)

Historical Note: Pavlov's work as a physiologist centered on digestive activity, and for this work he received the Nobel Prize in medicine in 1904. In his laboratory in Petrograd (now Leningrad), he first noticed secretion to "incidental" stimuli, which he then investigated and reported on in *Conditioned Reflexes* and later work.

PANEL R-7-2

F. S. Keller and W. N. Schoenfeld give the following account of an experiment by G. V. Anrep, one of Pavlov's pupils. The experiment was reported in 1920. Once again, the subject was a dog, and the salivary reflex was studied.

In this study, a tone of 637.5 cycles per second was sounded for a 5-second stimulation period; 2 or 3 seconds later the dog was given biscuit powder. At intervals of 5 to 35 minutes, this pairing was repeated. In 16 days, 50 such combinations were presented and 6 tests were made with the tone alone. The test tone was of 30 seconds' duration, and Anrep measured response magnitude by the number of drops of saliva that were secreted in this period. In addition, he recorded the latencies of the response, in seconds.

The results of the experiment are recorded in the table.

ACQUISITION OF A CONDITIONED SALIVARY REFLEX

Number of Paired Stimulations	Response Magnitude (drops of saliva)	Response Latency (seconds)
1	0	—
10	6	18
20	20	9
30	60	2
40	62	1
50	59	2

(*From:* Keller, F. S., and Schoenfeld, W. N., *Principles of Psychology.* New York: Appleton-Century-Crofts, 1950, p. 18.)

PANEL R-9-1

The following is another description of an experiment done by Pavlov in his laboratory:

1. A light is made a conditioned stimulus for salivation. This is accomplished in the following manner. The dog is put into a dark room, and at a certain moment a bright light is switched on. We wait for half a minute, and then give the dog food and allow it to eat for half a minute. This procedure is repeated several times. Finally the electric light, which at first was an indifferent agent for the animal, and had no relation whatever to the function of the salivary gland, owing to repeated coincidence of eating with salivary activity, becomes endowed with the property of acting as a special stimulus for the salivary gland. Every time the electric light appears we have a salivary secretion. Now we can say that the light has become a conditioned stimulus of the gland. The activity of the salivary gland in such a case serves as a simple reflex of the animal to the external world. This reflex gradually grows until it finally attains a certain limit, in the present case, ten drops of saliva in half a minute.

2. Now we add to the light a definite tone (of about 426 cycles per second). The combination of light and tone lasts a half minute. This combination of stimuli is never accompanied by feeding. For the first few applications of this combination there is no change in the original effect of the light, i.e., the light plus tone gives the same salivary secretion as the light alone did (ten drops in half a minute). I wish to emphasize that this combination is never accompanied by food. And after four or five applications of this combination (without feeding), the tone had acquired the property of acting as a stimulus of the salivary secretion. It is true the effect was very small, only one or two drops.

3. It is evident that the tone acquired its exciting effect by being applied simultaneously with the light, and it has actually gone through the same process as occurred when the light received (from its association with eating) its stimulatory effect on the salivary secretion. In the action of the tone we see the action of a new conditioned reflex, and as in the given case the effect of the tone came about owing to its coincidence with a conditioned stimulus (light) and not to coincidence with an unconditioned stimulus (food), this new stimulator (tone) can be designated as a stimulus of the second order, and the new reflex as a *reflex of the second order*. This effect, it is necessary to note, is in most cases very weak, only one or two drops, very transitory, and not fixed. If the experiments are continued for some time, the tone will lose its action. The secretory action itself is so small and it requires such exact conditions for its manifestation, that doubt may arise even as to its very existence.

(*Adapted from:* Pavlov, I. P., *Lectures on Conditioned Reflexes.* New York: International Publishers, 1928, pp. 104-105.)

PANEL O-2-1

Below is a typical experimental chamber for a pigeon.

The *keys* are usually translucent disks onto which colors or designs can be projected. A peck on the key closes a switch and records the occurrence of a response. Behind the *food aperture* is a metal box containing grain. This food tray can be raised for a second or two, providing the pigeon with access to food (grain) after a key peck. Then it drops below the aperture so that the pigeon can no longer reach the grain.

During experimentation the box is enclosed in a soundproof outer chamber.

PANEL O-2-2

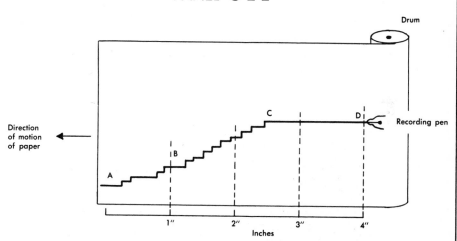

Above is pictured a section of the paper from the surface of the rotating drum on which are recorded the responses of key-pecking by the pigeon. The responses are recorded in a *cumulative* manner; that is, each time a response is made, the pen running across the paper on the drum makes a slight step upward. When no responses are being made, the pen moves in a straight line. Note that the pen never moves downward, only upward.

PANEL O-2-3

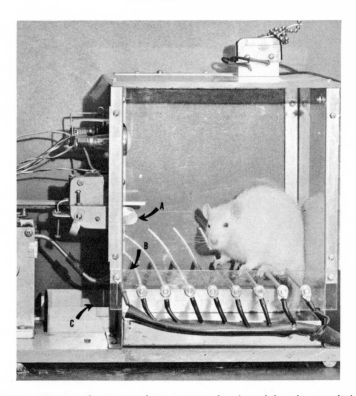

Above is a picture of a type of apparatus developed by the psychologist B. F. Skinner. This apparatus (technically known as the free operant apparatus) consists of a chamber in which the subject, a rat, can move about freely when placed in it. On the wall at the left is located a lever or bar (Point A) that can be pressed downward if the rat exerts a small force. Below the lever is located a water dipper (Point B) that can be activated to produce a drop of water from the tray below (Point C) whenever the rat pushes the bar. The dipper drops into the reservoir tray and brings up a drop of water. Each lever press response is automatically recorded. When water is presented after each bar press, the response rate increases.

(See: Godcharles, C. and Stebbins, W. C., "A Student Laboratory for Operant Conditioning," Journal Exp. Analysis of Behavior, 1962, 5, pp. 457-459.)

PANEL O-2-4

Conditioning Children

A large metal lever was mounted on one wall of an experimental playroom. Beneath the lever was an enamel tray into which candy could be dropped through a chute. The subjects were preschool children. The children were brought into the room (which contained a few toys) and left there. Each time they pressed the wall lever, a piece of candy fell into the food tray below.

RESULTS FOR ONE SUBJECT:

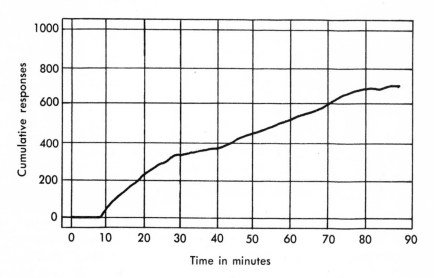

(From: Warren, A. Bertrand, and Brown, Robert H., "Conditioned Operant Response Phenomena in Children," J. Gen. Psychol., 1943, 28, pp. 181-207.)

PSYCHOLOGY I

TERMINAL EXAMINATION

1. *Reflex Conditioning*

1. What two things are necessary to make up a reflex?

    a. _____

    b. _____

2. DEFINE terms *a.* and *b.* and DESCRIBE how they are related in a reflex.

    a. _____

    b. _____

3. If stimulus intensity is increased, response magnitude

    ☐ increases

    ☐ decreases

    If stimulus intensity is increased, response latency

    ☐ increases

    ☐ decreases

    CHOOSE the correct relationship:

	Response magnitude		*Response latency*	
stimulus intensity	☐ direct	☐ inverse	☐ direct	☐ inverse
number of pairings	☐ direct	☐ inverse	☐ direct	☐ inverse

4. DEFINE:

    Threshold _____

    Subliminal stimulus _____

    Supraliminal stimulus _____

5. If a stimulus is weak the response it elicits would have a (☐ long ☐ short) latency and a (☐ strong ☐ weak) magnitude.

6. DRAW and LABEL the paradigm for an unconditioned reflex.

To what technical term does the arrow refer? _____

7. The title of a psychological study often states the dependent and independent variables. In each of the titles below UNDERLINE the dependent variable with one line and the independent variable with two lines.

   a. A study of the effect on muscular coordination in typewriting as a function of various amounts of alcohol drunk previously.

   b. The effect of various drugs upon patterns of web-weaving by a spider.

   c. Does lack of light in infancy affect visual ability in later life?

   d. Is fear (cringing, crying, etc.) in a young chimpanzee reduced when the chimpanzee's mother is present in the cage?

   e. What are the color patterns necessary to set off aggression in the Siamese fighting fish?

   f. The effects of continued test trials on a second order reflex.

   g. Changes in the latency of a conditioned reflex as a function of number of pairings between the CS and the US.

8. What is the major difference between an unconditioned and a conditioned stimulus? _____

9. Briefly describe the procedure you would use to make a reflex in which a handshake produced salivation. (Use a diagram if you find it helpful.) _____

10. *a.* What is the name of the procedure of pairing an unconditioned and a neutral stimulus? _____

b. What is the result of this procedure? _____

11. In a reflex conditioning experiment, how would you demonstrate that the conditioned stimulus was originally neutral? _____

12. As conditioning progresses

  a. The latency of the response to the CS

    ☐ increases

    ☐ decreases

  b. The magnitude of the response to the CS

    ☐ increases

    ☐ decreases

13. *a.* DESCRIBE the procedure of higher order conditioning by the use of an example. _____

b. WRITE the paradigms involved using the stimuli and response from your example. _____

14. What are the three types of Pavlovian conditioning procedures which depend on the CS ⟶ US interval?

  a. _____

  b. _____

  c. _____

Briefly describe the differences between these procedures.

_____

'. Operant Conditioning

1. A cumulative response curve shows the total number of _____ as a function of _____.

2. Which of these curves shows the highest rate of response? Which shows the lowest rate?

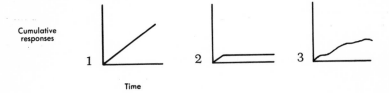

3. In the first 10 minutes of an experiment, an animal made 21 responses and in the last 10 minutes he emitted 87 responses. His response rate increased during the experiment from _____ to _____.

4a. DRAW two paradigms for operant conditioning contingencies.

b. Now, translate these two paradigms into words. _____

5. Define operant level. Why is it important to determine operant level? _____

6. Describe the procedure for testing whether a given stimulus is a reinforcer. _____

7. What are the two basic types of reinforcers, and how is each employed in strengthening operant behavior?

_____

_____

8a. What procedure do we use for developing an entirely new response? _____

b. Briefly describe this procedure. _____

9. To which of the following organisms does the principle of operant conditioning apply?
   ☐ aardvark
   ☐ bat
   ☐ cat
   ☐ dog
   ☐ elephant
   ☐ man
   ☐ pigeon
   ☐ quail
   ☐ squirrel
   ☐ whale

10. Give two ways in which operant and reflex procedures differ.
   a. _____
   b. _____

11. MATCH the following by writing in the most appropriate letter for each numbered item.

a. unconditioned stimulus

b. conditioned stimulus

c. subliminal stimulus

d. supraliminal stimulus

e. positive reinforcing stimulus

f. negative reinforcing stimulus

g. neutral stimulus

1. _____ a stimulus which acquires the power to elicit a response

2. _____ a stimulus whose presentation increases the strength of the response producing it

3. _____ a stimulus which elicits a response without training

4. _____ a stimulus whose termination may strengthen a response

5. _____ a stimulus which elicits no response

12. Which of the following could be considered examples of conditioning by removal of an S^{-R}?

☐ scratching an itch

☐ closing a window on a cold night

☐ trembling on a cold night

☐ throwing a ball

☐ putting up your umbrella in the rain

☐ punishing a child

☐ blushing with embarrassment

13. Give two ways in which reflex conditioning and escape conditioning are different.

14. After each of the following responses, indicate whether the response is an operant (by placing an O after the word) or a part of a reflex (by placing an R after the word).

     salivating ———

     walking ———

     key pecking ———

     reading ———

     blushing ———

     pupillary contraction ———

15. Set up an experiment to demonstrate the following:

A pigeon can learn bar-pressing when the bar-pressing response in the pigeon is nonexistent. The pigeon has never been used for an experiment before. Assume the bird has been trained to take food from the aperture. In your experimental procedure, include:

     precondition of the bird

     operant level

     the reinforcer

     shaping

     measures of conditioning

     paradigm

Why do you think such an experiment would be successful or unsuccessful?